On the Unseriousness
of Human Affairs

On the Unseriousness of Human Affairs

Teaching, Writing, Playing, Believing, Lecturing, Philosophizing, Singing, Dancing

James V. Schall

ISI Books
Wilmington, Delaware
2001

Copyright © 2001 ISI Books

Cataloging-in-Publication Data:

Schall, James V.
      On the unseriousness of human affairs : teaching, writing, playing, believing, lecturing, philosophizing, singing, dancing / by James V. Schall. — 1st ed. — Wilmington, Del. : ISI Books, 2001.

      p. ; cm.

      Includes bibliographical references and index.
      ISBN 1-882926-63-3
            1. Political science — Philosophy. 2. Christianity and politics. I. Title.

JA71 .S33 2001   2001-87757
320/ .01 — dc21   CIP

Book design by Sam Torode

Published in the United States by:

    ISI Books
    Post Office Box 4431
    Wilmington, DE 19807-0431

Manufactured in the U.S.

ACKNOWLEDGMENTS

I WISH TO THANK the following publishers for permission to use materials previously appearing in their journals: *The Academy*, Chapter 3, Interlude IV; *American Benedictine Review*, Chapter 1; The American Maritain Association, Chapter 4; *Crisis*, Interludes III and V; *Fellowship of Catholic Scholars Quarterly*, Chapter 6; *Midwest Chesterton News*, Interlude I; *Modern Age*, Chapter 5; *Perspectives in Political Science*, Chapter 8; *The Shakespearean Rag*, Interlude II; *Social Justice Review*, Chapter 2; *Vital Speeches*, Chapters 7, 9, and 11.

"Another thing to observe when you judge whether a nature is philosophic or not: be sure it has no slavishness in it. Nothing is so inimical as pettiness to a soul that always strives to reach the whole of everything human and divine."

"Most true," said Glaucon.

"Do you suppose a mind endowed with grandeur and the ability to view all time and all being can think much of the human life?"

"Impossible."

— PLATO, *Republic*

It must be borne in mind that no single existing thing is entirely deprived of participation in the Beautiful, for, as the true Word says, all things are very beautiful. Holy Contemplation can therefore be derived from all things.

— DIONYSIUS THE AREOPAGITE, *The Celestial Hierarchy*

Not only does the beauty I beheld
Transcend ourselves, but truly I believe
Its maker only may enjoy it all.

— DANTE, *Divine Comedy*

We then fell into a disquisition whether there is any beauty independent of utility. The General [Paoli] maintained there was not. Dr. Johnson maintained that there was; and he instanced a coffee-cup which he held in his hand, the painting of which was of no real use, as the cup would hold the coffee equally well if plain; yet the painting was beautiful.

— JAMES BOSWELL, *Life of Samuel Johnson*

Yet some things there are that they [the Ainur] cannot see, neither alone nor taking counsel together; for to none but himself has Ilúvatar revealed all that he has in store, and in every age there come forth things that are new and have no foretelling, for they do not proceed from the past.

— J. R. R. TOLKIEN, *The Silmarillion*

Contents

Introduction

MUCH WILL BE FOUND in this book about unexpected things, about gifts and surprises, about things that seem most important but which are held here to be "unserious"—and "unserious" is taken to be a compliment. Often in these pages, I will talk about the importance of "wasting" our time. I will suspect that it is quite possible not to learn much in our universities, at least not much about what is ultimately significant. I want to know what to "do" when all else is "done." To what does our "liberal learning" point? Merely to ourselves? How rarely do we wonder about these things! Indeed, not to wonder about them is almost the classical definition of what it is to be "illiberal."

What must be called the "mystery" of teaching and learning will often be pondered here. There will be praise for the short essay, so much so that it will help form the structure of the book itself: five short essays, which I call "interludes," are included between sundry chapters, partly to state things clearly, partly to change the pace of what is being argued. I am likewise fascinated with the prospect of finding seminal books, even of finding them inadvertently in some library or used bookstore. Almost every chapter contains striking passages that I have chanced to read and have not been able to put aside until I wrote them down. Thus, the structure of this book is leisurely, to some degree conversational. Truth, in fact, can only exist in conversation, to recall an observation of Plato.

But though this book's tone is informal, it is about ultimate things and their status among us. We do not much talk about these things, I know. But how ironical, never to consider what is of the highest moment! It is not that our modern preoccupation with politics and economics is a bad thing. Rather, this book points to the fact that these disciplines and realities will not be well-ordered unless we have some sense both of our own order, our "self-discipline," and of what is beyond them. What is beyond is something we have largely forgotten or, more likely, rejected. The "radical" nature of this book, the essence of which is emphasized by the centrality of the word "unserious," is the effort to reaffirm the truth of the central tradition of our culture: man is not the highest thing in existence even though his being, as such, is good—and it is good to *be*. Recognizing this truth does not lessen human dignity but enhances it.

I have placed at the beginning of the book five classic citations that, to me, guide the spirit of what is written here. One is from Plato, one from Dionysius, one from Dante, one from Boswell, and one from Tolkien. I suggest that, before reading anything in this book, the reader take some time to reflect on each of these passages. In effect, they exhort us, remind us about things we must consider if we would be whole. Thus, we seek to know if our nature is philosophic. Do we know our place in reality? Things are connected, including human things. Any thing, if we think deeply enough about it, can lead us to everything. For instance, when we know a beautiful thing, including a beautiful human thing, something worthy in itself, we reach beyond ourselves; indeed, we are *called* beyond ourselves. We do some things just because they are beautiful. Nor are all things merely repetitions of the past. The new really occurs.

The reader will find many of my friends in this book, both friends that I know and, as I try to suggest in Chapter 5, many whom I have never met, yet know through reading, through having been taught about them and by them. I do not hesitate to cite Charlie Brown and Lucy Van Pelt as philosophical authorities alongside real heroes like Aristotle, Augustine, G. K. Chesterton, Samuel Johnson, Josef Pieper, and many others with whom the reader, I hope, will become familiar.[1] I cite these diverse authorities to help me show that the highest things have a certain lightsomeness about them. We sometimes confuse ourselves by thinking that solemn things cannot also be joyful things. But Chesterton once remarked that he did not see why something that is true could not also be funny. There is no reason to separate gaiety from significance. The truth *is* joyful. The being of things is ultimately rooted in delight, in a delight that we do not "make" but discover to be already there, to be somehow given to us.

The subtitle of this book—*Teaching, Writing, Playing, Believing, Lecturing, Philosophizing, Singing, Dancing*—will, at first sight, seem odd. Each word is, of course, intended to point to some aspect of the leisured or "unserious" life that we are asked to live. Such things exist in our freedom and in our enchantment. Leon Kass, in a remarkable book, *The Hungry Soul: Eating and the Perfecting of Our Nature*, has shown how the most basic aspects and needs of our nature are eventually transformed into something higher, into something that exists at a more rare and delightful level.[2] We are, no doubt, wont to speak of "serious teaching" or "serious work," "serious writing" or even "serious play." Yet, we are told by Plato that our lives are not particularly serious. Actually, what Plato had in mind was something most profound: our lives have a certain importance, but only in the light of the seriousness of God.

Thus, the highest things, even prayer and belief, require a certain playfulness about them. It is only when we realize that human affairs stand not simply by themselves but relate us to our end—to our transcendent destiny—that we can relax about what we are, indeed, *become* what we are. What is written here is intended to direct us, or better perhaps to "re-direct" us, in those activities that naturally belong to us. Throughout the book, the theme recurs: what is it about our lives that makes them worth living?

Because the author of this book is a teacher, the reader need not be surprised that teaching and learning, and their impediments, often come up here. The author is also a Catholic and a priest. Of course, one need not apologize for what he is. But one needs to account for why things are of interest to him. Things Catholic rather make sense to me. I have read the arguments against what I hold. They are interesting and need to be reckoned with. If I am not convinced by them, it is only because I find them unconvincing. On the other hand, if things do make sense, it seems right to make the case for them. If there is any ultimate intellectual cause of unbelief, I have often thought, it is because there is too much delight and joy, not too little, in the world. For many, the evil in the world overshadows the good, obscures it, and even causes its denial. But it is the fact of joy that is the real mystery of our being.

This book is written, then, against the background of something that "need" not exist: the world itself and ourselves within it. We are, but we need not be. That this "not-needing-to-exist" is rather the best thing about us, that we need *not* exist but *do*—this is the theme of this book. The highest things cannot be such that, in their pursuit, we are deprived of the joy in which they "rest," to use a word that Augustine was fond of. How to go about speaking of these things? What I attempt here is a beginning. I want to provide a way of seeing and speaking about the highest things. Our human affairs are not "slavish," as Plato reminded us. We are free in their pursuit. Yes, it is quite likely, as Dante intimated, that only our "maker" can fully enjoy it all. Yet, that tiny portion of the highest things that we can enjoy, as Aristotle says, is worth all our time and effort (*Ethics*, X, 1105b30–1178a1).

This book, then, stands in the spirit of that philosopher who, in the *Republic*, finally "turned around" to realize that what he had considered real and serious was not so. Like Plato, we must take a certain initial step, one which allows us finally to realize that our major task is not to make our world but to respond to a reality *that is*. How do we respond? How else but by telling others about it, and by singing, dancing, even making offerings and praising a world in which we finally realize that our own lives have a certain "seriousness," to be sure, but are nothing compared to the reality to which we are open but which we do not make. It is this which causes us finally to "go out of ourselves," to be what we really are because we realize that we cannot be "self-sufficient." "In every age," as Tolkien said, "there come forth things that are new and have no foretelling." This is why human affairs are ultimately "unserious," for we do not "control" all that we are. We remain beings to whom much is given, including our openness to the highest things. The fact that we realize, with Dante, that "the maker" may be the only one to "enjoy it all" only means that our own joy exists in a freedom that makes the affairs that so absorb us seem utterly "unserious" by comparison.

Contrary to writers from Epicurus and Marx, the world need not be lessened by our attention to the highest things. Indeed, unless we know and strive for what is serious beyond our own enterprises, we will end up making the world our god, a role for which it was not intended.

❧

CHAPTER I

Ludere Est Contemplari:
On the Unseriousness of Human Affairs

I

ON APRIL 3, 1776, James Boswell and Samuel Johnson dined at the Mitre Tavern, where they engaged in discussion with John Murray, the solicitor general of Scotland. Murray, it seems, had "praised the ancient philosophers for the candor and good humor with which those of different sects disputed with each other." To this observation, Johnson responded:

> Sir, they disputed with great humor because they were not in earnest with regard to religion. Had the ancients been serious in their belief, we should not have had their Gods exhibited in the manner we find them represented in the Poets. The people would not have suffered it. They dispute with good humor on their fanciful theories, because they are not interested in the truth of them.[1]

What is "serious," Johnson intimated, is our relation to the gods, "the truth of them." About what is not serious, evidently, we can have a certain lightsome, genteel discussion, but this does not include the gods. Many

Greek philosophers, on the other hand, thought that religion merely supplied a kind of civic quietness to people who could not understand the seriousness of philosophy, of contemplation.

Let me begin these reflections with two further statements, one from St. Paul on running, the second of my own composition. The first reads: "Brothers, I do not think of myself as having reached the finish line. I give no thought to what lies behind but push on to what is ahead. My entire attention is on the finish line as I run toward the prize to which God calls me—life on high in Christ Jesus" (Phil. 3:12–15). The second, in Latin, reads simply, *Ludere est contemplari*—"to play is to contemplate"—or perhaps what I mean is, "to watch play is to contemplate." The two passages are connected in my mind because, in his *Politics*, Aristotle suggests that oftentimes the closest we come to contemplation in our lives is when we play. And neither play nor contemplation can be, strictly speaking, necessary.

We are familiar with St. Paul's analogy about running and attaining our ultimate goal. But such a sentence—"to play is to contemplate"—is not, as we might expect on first hearing it, a famous statement from a classical author, say Cicero or Aristotle. Rather it is, as it were, a "play" on the great Benedictine motto, *Laborare est orare*—"to work is to pray." No doubt, at first sight, it is much easier to associate work with prayer than it is to associate play with contemplation. I believe, however, it is only in modern times and because of certain modern intellectual assumptions about human autonomy that we prefer to associate prayer with work, not play. We have the *illusion*—a word itself connected with the Latin word, *ludere*, meaning "to play"—that what we are about is to make a world and not to receive a salvation. We think work obviously to be serious but play and the deeds of leisure to be frivolous, or at least unnecessary.

However, for Aristotle the most interesting and fascinating thing about play was precisely that it was "unnecessary." More than anything else, this freedom is what made play noble, what made it like contemplation, which Aristotle considered to be the highest act we could engage in and to which we should devote all the time and energy we can. And both play and prayer are important to the degree that they are unnecessary, to the degree that we are not constrained to do them. It is of some interest, I suggest, to think through why this might be so.

As Aristotle hinted in his discussion of art, this mysterious "unnecessity" is also characteristic of beautiful things, things to be made not for use, or not only for use, but to be seen or to be heard—just seen or heard. Beauty, as such, is not useful; yet, without it, we would not be what we are. This is why a religion indifferent to beauty is a religion indifferent to the real end for which we are made. And yet, as St. Augustine told us, we can find in the beautiful things that God made a reason not to seek, not to "run after," as St. Paul put it, God Himself. It is as possible for us to avoid beauty by beauty as it is for us to find intimations of divine beauty through finite beauty, something most memorably spelled out for us in Plato's *Symposium.* In the highest things, we are free. This is why we can miss the suggestions of divine beauty in the finite things of this world, why we can lose the race, why we might think that something finite is enough for us.

To a great extent, modernity has dedicated itself to the laudable task of redeeming work, allowing the things that slaves used to do to become ways to civil dignity and eternal salvation. We should remember that in the ancient world a person was a slave not so much because of his birth or his legal status but because of the servile nature of his work. The oppressive nature of much of this work is why Aristotle could propose that with the invention of machines most of the slavery that did not involve complete lack of intelligence would be eliminated. No doubt, the very fact that St. Joseph was a carpenter and Christ his Son was enough for Christianity to reverse the ancient understanding of work as such, or better, its understanding of the worker. We are still in danger, however, of identifying humanity with its work rather than its highest activities.

Like Benjamin Franklin in his *Autobiography,* we associate work with serious purpose. The New Testament also related working to a serious purpose—he who will not work, neither let him eat. Even "recreation," which for Aristotle means a respite to go back to work more efficiently, is an academic "major" in many universities; that is, it is a preparation for a certain kind of work. And we do not have to reduce work to the status of slavery to deny that, however worthy, it is not the highest thing we can do. On the other hand, something abiding is found in Aristotle's remark that recreation is related to work, while sport or play is closer to contemplation than is business or labor or even politics.

II

There are many ways to illustrate the contrast between modernity's notion of the autonomy and primacy of worldly affairs and the older, classical, Judeo-Christian view of the primacy of the higher things. For instance, my sister-in-law, in reading Barbara Tuchman's book *A Distant Mirror*, noted a passage that I think is pertinent in light of a monastic tradition that dates back to the sixth century. This Benedictine tradition has stood for precisely the primacy of contemplation, even when the very words *peace* and *work* and *beauty* were most directly associated with its self-description and of the atmosphere it created within itself.

"Difficulty of empathy, of genuinely entering into the mental and emotional values of the Middle Ages, is the final obstacle (to understanding them)," writes Tuchman:

> The main barrier, I believe, is the Christian religion as it then was: the matrix and law of medieval life, omnipresent, indeed compulsory. Its insistent principle that the life of the spirit and of the afterworld was superior to the here and now, to material life on earth, is one that the modern world does not share, no matter how devout some present day Christians may be. The rupture of this principle and its replacement by belief in the worth of the individual and of the active life not necessarily focused on God is, in fact, what created the modern world and ended the Middle Ages.[2]

Christianity does, of course, hold that "the life of the spirit and of the afterworld" is superior to our life on earth. Tuchman implies that if this priority were taken seriously, we would not have the advantages of modernity.

Stanley Jaki, on the other hand, argues that without this particular Christian concept of God, the modern world's scientific basis would not be possible at all.[3] Likewise, defenders of Christianity hold that the Greek doctrine of the immortality of the soul and the Christian doctrine of the Resurrection of the body are really the positions that have contributed most to the notion of "the worth of the individual." In any case, the issue is joined. Christianity and modern civilization are here placed in apparent opposition at their most essential points, even though Christianity is the one system that joins, through its doctrine of the Incarnation, both the life of the spirit and the life of this world in one coherent whole. In this sense, I think, the implications of Barbara Tuchman's remark are, to some degree, anti-Christian. To be Christian is not to emphasize the life of the spirit in such a way that the world does not exist, nor to exalt the worldly enterprise in such a way that higher concerns are inimical to what it means to live on earth. Medieval people *did* hold that individuals have ultimate worth and that their daily lives are intended to include the admonitions of the faith.

In times of wars and rumors of war, which I suppose may be any time in some part of the world, I know it will seem strange, even a bit improper, to talk of play and not of peace or victory or protest. Perhaps this very impropriety itself is a good reason to speak about play and leisure, lest we become too absorbed in what we must admit is the fascination of war. We are frequently told that "the drama of war is inescapable." This is the same fascination, as we shall see, of which Plato himself was aware. It is a fascination that indeed seems to make human things more important than they really are. Yet, in the Christian tradition, peace is never really something we set out to accomplish or obtain as if it were something we could have independently of other virtues or activities. We set out to accomplish order and dignity and fairness and productivity. We think these are real attributes of existence and not figments of our imaginations. The abstract crying out for peace and more peace is not a way to achieve it but a way mostly not to find it. Peace is not a *thing* alongside other things but a result, a "tranquility of order," as Saint Augustine called it. If we have no order, especially inner order, we have no peace.

A man or woman joins the Benedictine Order, as I take it, not in order to achieve some thing or some good called "peace." Rather, each one enters into a place where order exists, the order of the day, where the virtues and the sacrifices are practiced. These exercises and duties are the things that everyone "works" at, the things that each does. Peace is a kind of result, almost an afterthought. Peace is the result of doing the right things, of attending to the highest things. But again, both the worst and the best human orders produce "peace," so it makes a difference on what basis the order of things is established. Beelzebub's kingdom is not divided against itself. The devil has his own order, as does the land of the tyrant, an order that produces a kind of "peace." It is for this reason that "war colleges" often make more sense than "peace academies."

For these reasons, perhaps, no phrase in modern spirituality or politics is more ironic or more dangerous than that of "working for peace." Strictly speaking, such a "work" is what we do not and cannot do. When the Lord said, "Be at peace, I have conquered the world," things about Him were from all external signs in chaos. If God's will among men cannot be accomplished until men have achieved peace, then it must simply follow that God's will is never done. Yet, we must maintain that God's will is being upheld even amidst our own social and personal disorder. His peace, as it were, exists in spite of all external chaos. This is another way of saying, I suppose, that what God is about and what men are about may not be the same thing.

In his question on the "Governance of Things," Saint Thomas observed: "For as 'it belongs to the best to produce the best,' it is not fitting that the supreme goodness of God should produce things without giving them their perfection. Now a thing's ultimate perfection consists in the attainment of its end. Therefore, it belongs to the Divine goodness, as it brought things into existence, so to lead them to their end...." (ST, I, 103, 1). If this passage means anything, it means that no external condition can ultimately interfere with our freely reaching our end. We are the only thing that can prevent it. The governance of God over His creation, His ability to bring it to its end, does not depend on the affairs of men, though it does include them. He is as present in our tragedies as in our elations. The Cross is, as à Kempis said, a way, a "royal road."

III

In the terms of political philosophy, I can put this point about God's power over good and evil situations in this way: men can be saved in the worst of regimes and damned in the best. Not only must human and divine freedom imply this consequence, but the criterion we choose for understanding one another must include this possibility. In titling this chapter "On the Unseriousness of Human Affairs," I mean to emphasize that the purpose of God in creation—that we might reach our end, that we might run to win the prize—is achieved in each of us, even if we choose ourselves over God. Our affairs do not determine our ends as if something outside of ourselves ruled our fate, let alone ruled God's governance of His creation. This truth does not mean that our affairs stand for nothing, or that our own salvation is not bound up with what we do or believe. But it does indicate that what is really "serious" lies behind the surface of human affairs and has to do with our achieving our divine purpose. If God has any problem with us, it has to do with our wills, not with our world, for it is in the human will where things go wrong.

The point is best illustrated in the conversation between the soldier Michael Williams and the disguised King Henry on the night before Agincourt. Ordinary soldiers are sitting around waiting for the battle at dawn. They think the king quietly sitting beside them is just another soldier. Williams reflects that if "the cause be not good, the king himself hath a heavy reckoning to make when all those legs and arms and heads, chopped off in a battle, shall join together at the latter day and cry all, 'We died at such a place,' some swearing, some crying for a surgeon.... I am afeared there are few die well that die in a battle..." (IV, i). Initially, Williams seeks to make someone else, preferably the king, responsible for his own internal status before God. The gore of battle is a good excuse for shunting this blame from oneself.

Henry, pretending to be just another soldier, challenges the position that he is responsible for the moral condition of his individual soldiers. Rather, he thinks, each soldier is responsible for his own faults. "Every subject's duty is the king's, but every subject's soul is his own," Henry affirms. To this, Williams, in the name of all common soldiers in all the armies of mankind, agrees, "'Tis certain, every man that dies ill, the ill is upon his own head—the king is not to answer it." The will of God is achieved for each individual in war no less than in peace. There are no external solutions to our relationship with God.

It is true that the end of war was always conceived to be peace, a tradition from Plato himself, and certainly from Saint Augustine. The most serious question we can confront, the most dangerous one, however, is not what we would do in war, but what we would do in peace. The real "war" only begins when the wars of battle are over. It is not without amusement and fascination that Plato began the discussion in the *Laws* with an account of how much old and young men could drink. Plato was not an advocate of Alcoholics Anonymous or a lush, and Socrates apparently could drink anyone under the table and show no signs of being out of control. But Plato would have understood the conversation of Henry and Williams. Plato was almost the first to realize that the activities of joy are more profound and more potentially dangerous than any war. The virtue of courage is the one that has to do with our staying alive or dying honorably. But it is prudence and the contemplative and supernatural virtues that have to do with our living well.

IV

When we are young, we begin to read war stories, adventure stories, and mystery stories; we are caught up in the world's failures, which we are sure we can correct. And therefore we are genuinely perplexed by what life has in store after the war is over, the adventure ended, and the mystery solved. It all seems so boring without the adventure of battle. We are told in romances that "they lived happily ever after," but this strikes us as meaning that the heroes and heroines had nothing left to do. What indeed is there left to do when all else, when all the serious things are done? Plato, in the seventh book of the *Laws*, gives a hint of what is in store for us.

On a day's walk to a religious shrine on Crete, the Athenian Stranger is speaking to Klinias, a local soldier and statesman. The Stranger had just told the old gentleman from Crete that only God is worthy of serious attention. Man is not the "measure of all things," as the Greek philosopher Pythagoras had maintained and much of modern thought has echoed. Rather, man has been devised by God as a "plaything," an affirmation that sounds to us, on first hearing it, as it did to the two men listening to the Athenian, insulting. We are not prepared to hear our wars, economies, and policies so denigrated. The Athenian Stranger goes on to affirm, as if to emphasize the point, that the fact that man is a mere plaything of God is indeed the "best" thing about him (803c).

Klinias does not quite understand this perplexing remark. Indeed, Klinias is very modern. The whole modern argument against God is that He has distracted us from the really important things—our own lot, our own making of a world that is ours alone to redeem, our efforts to make the world safe for democracy, our drive to alleviate poverty and sickness and even death. Anything devoted to the transcendent is so much distraction. Indeed, religion is not merely the opium of the people, but the rival of man. We are not free if we worship a God who has made us an image or a plaything. For if it is possible we might not have existed at all, then we cannot be so important. Freedom, for us, means not only having no golden strings attached to us guiding us to the right action but also not even having instructions as to what a human being *is*. The opposition to God is therefore presented to us as exhilarating, humanistic, confidence-giving, all-absorbing, and yes, serious. We can begin to be "serious" about ourselves, it seems, only when God is dead, and, as Nietzsche added, we are the ones who killed Him.

The Athenian's response to this worry about the downgrading of human importance contains the essence of what I want to emphasize here:

> Nowadays, presumably, they [the people] suppose the serious things are for the sake of the playful things, for it is held that the affairs pertaining to war, being serious matters, should be run well for the sake of peace. But the fact is that in war there is not and will not be by nature either play or, again, an education that is at any time worthy of our discussion; yet this is what we assert is for us, at least, the most serious thing. Each person should spend the greatest and best part of his life in peace. What then is the correct way? One should live out one's days playing at certain games—sacrificing, singing, and dancing.... (803 d–e)

Plato identifies sacrifice, song, and dance not only with play, but also with what a person should spend most of his life doing.

Sacrifice, song, and dance, then, are what we should be doing to honor God in times of peace. That is to say, at peace, we should be about ritual, about what is done that need not be done, about what is beautiful that need not be, about what exists that need not exist at all. This activity is what we should be about. Plato recalls that same teaching found in the early myths about the founding of the muses and the origins of the world. The gods had looked about after they had created everything perfectly to wonder if anything was left out. And they found, in a marvelous insight, that there was no one to praise what was created, and so we have the muses, the inspirations of song, poetry, dance, and the arts.

To this quite astonishing presentation of what is important in human affairs, the Spartan Megillus, the third participant in the conversation that took place on the way to Knossos that midsummer afternoon, protested to the Athenian, "Stranger, you are belittling our human race in every way." Surely nothing is more important than human affairs, and of course war, business, and the affairs of the city are the real human affairs. For mankind longs to have something important to do that is its own, something not dependent on anything but itself.

The Athenian Stranger realized the perplexity of his two companions. He knew that to say that human affairs are really quite unserious, quite unimportant in the order of things, would seem so outlandish, so extreme, that what he was saying could not be understood. So he said to the Spartan gentleman: "Don't be amazed, Megillus, but forgive me! For I was looking away toward God and speaking under the influence of that experience when I said what I did just now. So let our race be something that is not lowly then, if that is what you cherish, but worthy of a certain seriousness" (804b). Notice what is said here. The Stranger realized that poor Megillus was a good politician, a soldier, from a good city. The Stranger had not meant that human affairs were of no seriousness at all, but compared to the "madness" of the divine breaking into each person's world, they were relatively insignificant. The Stranger did not intend to say that the affairs of the world were nothing. He meant something even more wondrous: that the affairs of God were infinitely greater than the most fascinating of human affairs.[4]

Plato had never forgotten that the politicians killed the philosopher. The philosopher finally had to set up a city in speech, if he were to live in harmony with those who had power, a city that Saint Augustine later on saw could only come from revelation. But the purpose of philosophy, at its best, was to teach something of the contemplative life to the politician who was so busy with worldly enterprises that he did not know what was really important in human affairs. Was there a way to do this? Both Plato and Aristotle thought that music and poetry would help. They both understood the importance of play, of something done for its own sake, something that was worth watching for itself. The problem of contemplation was not to create God but to discover Him. And this discovery initially consisted in having at least some experience of freedom, of sheer fascination and delight that had no reward but itself.

"We have not made cricket and football professional because of any astonishing avarice or any new vulgarity," G. K. Chesterton wrote on August 25, 1906.

> We have made them professional because we would have them perfect. We have dedicated men to them as to some god of an inhuman excellence. We care more for football than for the fun of playing football. The modern Englishman cares more for cricket than for being a cricketer. And having taken the frivolous things seriously, we naturally take the serious things frivolously. Our Derby is the most important thing in England.[5]

I do not often disagree with Chesterton, but in this I do. The watching of a good game is not merely frivolous. Without getting into the question of the abuse of sports, I think that Chesterton was right in his basic point. We do like our sports "perfect." In caring more for watching a game of football than playing it, we attest, I think, to a kind of wonder, a kind of fascination about something taking place before us that absorbs our attention, if only for a moment.

Even Aristotle admitted that this moment of beholding was not "serious," but he knew it was free, for its own sake. I suspect that the sophisticated critics of spectatorship miss the real point about them. Good games and sporting events are the normal and symbolic experiences most people have that might teach them to understand something of God, to understand how something could be for its own sake. This experience teaches us how it is possible that something we might contemplate is something we might contemplate forever if it were forever fascinating.

V

The Feast Day of Saint Elizabeth Seton is January 4. To conclude the Office of that day, there is a brief conference that she gave to her sisters. In it, she asks them,

> What are our real trials? By what name shall we call them? One cuts herself out a cross of pride; another, one of causeless discontent; another, one of restless impatience or peevish fretfulness. But is the whole any better than children's play if looked at with the common eye of faith? Yet we know that our God calls us to a holy life, that he gives us every grace, every abundant grace; and though we are so weak of ourselves, this grace is able to carry us through every obstacle and difficulty.

Plato compared our lives to "playthings," while Mother Seton saw our sins and faults as mere "children's play" before the mystery of God. If we are given "every grace, every abundant grace," as she put it, does this not mean that human affairs cannot be "serious" but frivolous until they are seen in their intention, until they are seen in the light of God's vision, his watching of our deeds and hearts—our response to what is not of our own making?

Let me recall some basic themes of what I have been saying, themes that recall how our lives are noble precisely because, in Plato's sense, they are "unserious":

> "Is the whole any better than children's play?"

> "'Tis certain, every man that dies ill, the ill is upon his own head—the king is not to answer for it."

> "It belongs to the divine goodness, as it brought things into existence, so to lead them to their end."

> "Only God is worthy of serious attention."

"One should live out one's days playing at certain games—sacrificing, singing, and dancing."

"Stranger, you belittle the human race in every way."

"Don't be amazed, Megillus, but forgive me! For I was looking away toward God."

"I run to win the prize to which God calls me."

The unseriousness of human affairs is, to conclude, the consequence of understanding the primacy of God. Real things are not less because other real things are more. If the whole of what we do—if the whole world—is merely "child's play," as Plato also intimated, it is not because there is no drama among us. Rather, it is because we are already included in a drama of infinitely greater grandeur than anything we could possibly make or even imagine by ourselves.

Each of us has his own drama before God. God leads us—monks and soldiers, kings and paupers, the happy and the sad—to His own end. In this sense, we are equal. The secular world reduces our lives to the here and now or at best to a mere transcultural reality. It is true that we always must find ourselves in a here and now, in a place that is a particular place. But we reach forth for that which is transcendent. If "only God is worthy of serious attention," it is because no good less than He is worthy of us.

We respond to God best in the freest of our activities—Plato's sacrificing, singing, and dancing. We do not belittle our race when we acknowledge our real place in the order of things. We are important, yet God attracts and calls us. We seek the prize to which we are called, not the one we create for ourselves. When we find only ourselves, we find Hell. But when we find that we are made for a delight that already exists at the end of things, we find Joy.

CHAPTER 2

❦

On Teaching and Being Eminently Teachable

REMARKS ON TEACHING and being taught, or as I put it, being eminently teachable, need certain initial and provocative words to indicate the spirit in which the subject matter is being approached. Almost always, when thinking of these matters, I begin with Leo Strauss's remark that we are lucky if our lives coincide with those of one or two of the greatest human thinkers to ever live. And even if we are lucky enough to be contemporaries with a couple of the great thinkers, it is unlikely that we shall either meet them or recognize them for what they are. In this sense, the beginning of wisdom is a small dose of humility, of our willingness to acknowledge how much was known and learned before we ourselves ever were.

Consequently, if we are to confront the greatest minds, we must do so in their books, to which we must attend with the greatest care and respect. And we must begin with the firm conviction that the mind, including our own mind, is capable of knowing *all that is,* that it is *capax omnium.* What stands between us and Aristotle or Dante is not power, as we are often told. We can know what Aristotle or Dante held. But as Strauss cautioned, once we do begin to try to learn from the great thinkers—if begin is indeed what we choose to do—we will find that they often contradict one another. The great books or thinkers, in other words, are not, as is too often implied, substitutes for thought itself. We probably do not, moreover, have time in one lifetime adequately to encounter even one of these great thinkers.[1]

But we should not proceed from these initial remarks to the contemporary despair about mind itself. Rather we should again ponder that marvelous advice from the Tenth Book of Aristotle's *Ethics*, which reads: "We must not follow those who advise us, being men, to think of human things, and being mortal, of mortal things, but must, so far as we can, make ourselves immortal, and strain every nerve to live in accordance with the best thing in us; for even if it be small in bulk, much more does it in power and worth surpass everything" (1177b33–78a3). To follow Aristotle here requires considerable moral courage.

It is fair to say, I think, that in some basic sense the lowering of our sights, something characteristic of modernity has been based on a largely unsuccessful effort to prove Aristotle wrong. What modernity has often accomplished instead is to use its power and prestige to forbid us from understanding why Aristotle might have been, at the most fundamental level of wonder and being, right. My initial observation is that the single most important thing we can do to provoke students to want to learn is to confront them with Aristotle's challenge, his reminder that the pursuit of the highest things, however difficult, is worth the effort and "surpasses everything."

I cite these magnificent, exalted lines of Aristotle, let me caution you, having read the following sober lines from Wesley McDonald, lines mindful of Allan Bloom's observation that what any professor today can be absolutely certain of is that his students will be relativists:[2]

> My young classroom charges, although wholly ignorant of Mill, have absorbed unreflectively his platitudes about tolerance and equality. If they agree on any moral principle, it could be summarized simply as,

"You can do whatever pleases you as long as you don't bug me." They also believe, inconsistently like Mill, that government has the responsibility of guaranteeing more personal liberty while simultaneously bringing about greater equality. And social scientists confidently inform us that crime and social pathologies are mere manifestations of society's failure to eliminate ignorance entirely. Mill flattered the mass of people with the notion that they are rational and good. Such beliefs, even though all experience refutes them, operate ... strongly on the popular imagination....[3]

No one will seek the highest if he believes that there is no truth, that nothing is his fault, and that government will guarantee his wants.

Let me continue by citing three passages that give a sharp flavor to what I want to say about inciting and provoking students. The first comes from Yves Simon's moving reflection on what it is to be a teacher. Simon remarked that "no spontaneous operation of intellectual relations protects the young philosopher against the risk of delivering his soul to error by choosing his teachers infelicitously."[4] In essence, this passage says nothing more than that man is a social animal, that we are somehow bound together (for better and for worse), and that the life of the mind is not immune from its own form of corruption even in the most expensive universities and even at the hands of the most famous professors.

The second passage I will cite in the Latin of Thomas Aquinas. Remember in reading or listening to it, that the word *stultitia* means "foolishness." It is the very word we find in the Latin translation of 1 Corinthians 20, where St. Paul, speaking of the pride of the philosophers, asks, "Nonne stultam fecit Deus sapientiam hujus mundi? [Did God not make the wisdom of this world foolish?]." *Stultitia* is, in St. Thomas's view, the contrary of wisdom, itself both the highest of the theoretical virtues and the gift of the Holy Spirit.

This is what St. Thomas says: "Stultitia ... import quendam stuporem sensus in judicando, et praecipue circa altissimam causam, quae est finis ultimus et summum bonum" [Foolishness ... implies a certain paralysis of the senses in judging, and especially concerning the highest cause, which is the final end and highest good]" (ST, II-II, 46, 2). Thomas suggests here that the reason we do not reflect on the highest things—the reason why we do not know what we could about our ultimate end or highest good—is not, as Aristotle thought, because the human intellect is limited (though it is). Rather, we allow ourselves to be stupified, to be deflected by what are admittedly many interesting and absorbing things; we do not order our lives so that we are taken beyond what is before us.

The third passage I wish to cite is from the *Republic*, wherein Socrates makes my point in a more positive manner. The passage from the Fifth Book, posed in the form of a question, reads: "the one who is willing to taste every kind of learning with gusto, and who approaches learning with delight, and is insatiable, we shall justly assert to be a philosopher, won't we?" (475c). In a sense, the whole Platonic corpus is addressed to potential philosophers. With Plato, we are concerned with those whose souls are drawn to many and sundry things, but who do not yet know how they will choose. Thus, if I might put it this way, Simon warns us about our professors, Aquinas reminds us about ourselves, and Plato seeks to know what we delight in—whether it is in all things, the whole, and whether we are able in our hearts to be gladdened by something for its own sake.

The question of being teachable, then, concerns intellectual curiosity. How does one go about inspiring, cajoling, or inciting students or other inquisitive human types to take an interest and delight in the highest things? I would leave the issue formulated in that way except that the phrase "intellectual curiosity" contains some dangerous ambiguity. The point can be made by recalling that the devil is intellectually curious; indeed, from all reports, Lucifer is most intellectually curious, originally in fact an angel of brilliant light, as his name implies. Aristotle's gingerly treatment of Socrates' notion that vice or error was merely ignorance also betrays a certain wariness toward intellectual curiosity. So I am not so much interested in intellectual curiosity as I am in an intense desire to know the truth of things "with gusto," as Socrates said—even though, in one sense, knowing what the devil knows is also a part of knowing the truth of things.

The knowledge of error and vice, as Plato and St. Thomas have taught us, is itself good, itself an instrument of orderly education. Evil is not to be located in the intellect but in the will. Knowledge of error and vice is a necessary element in knowing the complete truth about anything. Aquinas wisely surrounded his famous proofs for the existence of God with the two most crucial arguments against such proofs, that from the existence of evil and that from the hypothesis that we can explain everything with our own intellects. And to make the point more forcefully, Aquinas proceeded to formulate these objections more concisely and accurately than anyone before or since has succeeded in doing. Indeed, no knowledge of truth is secure without an awareness of how multiple errors derive from and are related to truth.

And yet, as Simon intimated, we can deliver our souls to dangerous teachers; we can, and often do, call darkness light not just out of ignorance but because we embody evil and selfish choices in our lives and in our laws. As Augustine taught us, an element of will, indeed self-will, puts at risk every truth's capacity to be itself. Our will can obscure our very potential to affirm or judge of *what is* that *it is.* Or, as it is put positively, again in the Fifth Book of the *Republic,* "Doesn't knowledge naturally depend on what *is,* to know of what *is* that it is and how it is?" (477b). Should we choose to answer "no" to Socrates' very serious question, should we say that knowledge does not depend on our affirmation of *what is,* we can be sure our intellectual confusions run very deep.

How would we approach this particular issue about our wanting to know, about our wanting our minds to be conformed to reality, to *what is?* The *Wall Street Journal* editors did an interesting editorial on campus bookstores a few years back.[5] They discovered, much to their amusement, that the bestsellers in college bookstores were basically the same as those in airports. The editors, needless to say, did not think that this fact was particularly encouraging, though they did draw one positive conclusion: students were voluntarily reading romantic novels rather than frittering away their time with the politically correct tomes that so often dominate university curricula. Students may read the same common stuff that folks waiting for a flight to Toledo read, but at least they do not display that more dangerous trendiness found in the isolation of universities where, though there are quotas for everything else, there are no quotas for truth, for affirmations that *what is, is.*

I often think—though like everyone else I too have a computer that, with the flick of about twenty buttons, allows me to access the library catalogue of the University of Perugia—that the bookstores that will save civilization are not online, nor on campuses, nor named Borders, Barnes & Noble, Dalton, or Crown. They are the used bookstores, in which, for a couple of hundred dollars, one can still find, with some diligence, the essential books of our culture, from the Bible and Shakespeare to Plato, Augustine, and Pascal. But do today's students care? What seems to be missing—and we must remember that Plato himself thought this quality a rare thing—is that Socratic *eros* that is fascinated by reality, that is unsettled by our spiritual uneasiness and what the *Journal* called "the emphasis on feeling instead of reasoning." Higher education, education that transmits and reflects on the highest things, as I have tried to hint in my *Another Sort of Learning,* is today largely a matter of private enterprise, good fortune, and reading things that few assign or praise.[6]

By chance of late, I found an old copy of Evelyn Waugh's *Brideshead Revisited.* In the early pages of this remarkable novel—a work that unfolds something essential to the needs of our souls—we come across a young British officer by the name of Hooper. Hooper is described by Waugh as the "new man," meaning a man with none of the old illusions about human beings, society, or God. What is remarkable about Hooper is that nothing noble really moves him. Yes, Hooper had often "wept"; but, as Charles Ryder, the novel's hero, recalls, never for Henry's speech on St. Crispin's Day, nor for the epitaph at Thermopylae. The history they taught him had few battles in it but, instead, a profusion of detail about humane legislation and recent industrial change. Gallipoli, Balaclava, Quebec, Lepanto, Bannockburn, Roncevales, and Marathon—these, and the Battle in the West where Arthur fell, and a hundred such names whose trumpet-notes, even now...called to me irresistibly across the intervening years with all the clarity and strength of boyhood, sounded in vain to Hooper.[7]

This is still the issue, isn't it? Too often, ours is an insipid education consisting of details about supposedly humane, though mostly lethal, legislation, about technological change confused with wisps of environmentalist madness—nothing to move souls, no real causes, no real romance. C. S. Lewis had described this same phenomenon in *The Abolition of Man*.[8]

Are we not led to wonder, since the time of Charles Ryder's musings, whether our educational institutions have not been filled with succeeding generations of Hoopers happily impervious both to what is disordered in our hyper-politicized campuses and to the call of the higher things? Are not St. Crispin's Day and Lepanto still falling on deaf ears? Judging by the works sold in campus bookstores, the *Journal* editors concluded, students still seem strangely "enchanted" by "New-Age style wonderings." They roam to every place but to where the truth might be found.

An old scholastic adage used to say that truth is one but that error tends to multiplicity. It is a bewildering experience, no doubt, for a young man or woman to sit down for the first time and begin to read a university catalogue, to note the variety of subjects, courses, and entertainments that are found listed there. If in addition to this we add some awareness through the media, libraries, or Internet of the incredible variety of other things apparently available to be learned, we can see that the temptation to write it all off as hopeless is very great. Most are convinced that they have to have an "education," a word, when we think about its derivation, that implies no content, as if we could have an education without knowing something in particular.

St. John Bosco, a nineteenth-century Italian saint, was famous for founding schools primarily devoted to technical and practical education for those who did not want or who were not able to pursue more academic pursuits—the kind of education, I presume, that one supposedly received at the time in the Jesuit colleges. Don Bosco's was a clerical vision of the sort of truth one can learn by reading *Zen and the Art of Motorcycle Maintenance* or Eric Gill's explanation of his printing: if someone really learns how to make and take care of something well, he will learn about everything else. The same insight can be gleaned from a reading of Louis L'Amour's *Education of a Wandering Man*, from which it is clear that a gifted and curious man can get an education just by reading books—lots of books—year after year.[9]

In *A Place on Earth*, Wendell Berry tells of Jayber Crow, the local barber in Port William who grew up in the Good Shepherd orphanage. While there, he read every book in the library several times; then he went to college for a few years and read constantly there as well. Berry describes Jayber Crow as a man who was "vastly more inclined to learn than to be taught."[10] This quotation, I think, emphasizes the two basic elements in intellectual curiosity. First, we need to have a desire to learn, to learn "with gusto." Without this, no one can do much for us. Chesterton once remarked that there is no such thing as a boring subject; there are only bored people. Second, we need to be taught. Just as our inclination to learn is innate, our need to be taught is intrinsic to our nature and something that needs to be understood more clearly.

Both St. Augustine and St. Thomas have treatises entitled *De Magistro* ("On the Teacher"). But perhaps the most interesting passage in either of these saints' writings about how to learn, or how to be taught, is found in Aquinas's prologue to the *Summa Theologiae*. It is important to note that the *Summa* was written for beginners, for Plato's potential philosophers, as it were, for those who wanted to learn but did not quite know how to go about it.

With this purpose in mind, then, St. Thomas identified three reasons why students often found it difficult to learn, even when they wanted to. The first is rather amusing, reminiscent of the student who encounters the unending listings in a university catalogue and asks himself how he could learn about the important things in such a morass. Thus, Aquinas observed, a very useless multiplication of disparate and varying questions, articles, and arguments confront the young beginner. He is given, in short, everything from Zeno to Hegel, everything from the Tan Dynasty to the latest perspectives on black holes, and of course the newest views on racism, sexism, environmentalism, and otherism, all in one large jumble of unrelated information. Seeing no order of learning, wrote Aquinas, the beginner becomes confused and discouraged.

The second problem arises when those things which are required for knowing are not presented after the order of the discipline or subject itself but are instead presented simply according to the arbitrary structure of a book, topic of dispute, or conversation. In this case, one might understand the book or conversation but not how it relates to anything else. The key notion for St. Thomas was "ordo disciplinae"; that is, there is an order of subject and its parts, and of subjects themselves to one another. Seeing this order, however long it might take to master it, makes learning both delightful and easier.

Third, learning is difficult because the frequent disordered repetition of information without seeing its "ordo disciplinae" generates in the souls of the student what Aquinas amusingly, but correctly, calls "fastidium et confusionem," that is, loathing and confusion. Much of our difficulty in provoking students to learn, I think, arises precisely from the sense of loathing and confusion that naturally arises when they are confronted, as they usually are, with a mass of unrelated material.

In his discussion of the teacher, Aquinas is at pains to remind us of our own capacity to know. We can, like Jayber Crow or Louis L'Amour, learn by ourselves from reality. "Scientia, ergo, praeexistit in addiscente in potentia non pure passiva, sed activa; alius homo per seipsum non potest acquirere scientiam [Knowledge therefore preexists in the one knowing not in a purely passive, but in an active way; otherwise man would not be able to acquire knowledge]" (*De Veritate*, 11, 1). Quite clearly, we are capable of acquiring knowledge, even by ourselves. This is why, fortunately, knowledge of *what is* can develop almost anywhere there is an inquisitive mind wondering about the truth of things.

But for most of us, an orderly learning is far easier and more productive. With the aid of someone who knows already, who has been through all the mistakes one is likely to make, and who takes delight in truth, we can learn easily, provided we allow ourselves to be eminently teachable. Simon suggested that there are three kinds of students: those who are only interested in grades, those who constantly ask questions but are never willing to listen, and those who recognize that there are ways to learn that others know better than themselves. The first two types are simply not teachable, but the third recognizes that he must take responsibility for his education and has a certain faith or trust that someone else can guide him.

Thus, Aquinas remarks that "docens, qui explicite total scientiam novit, expeditius potest ad scientiam inducere quam aliquis induci possit ex seipso, per hoc quod cognoscit scientiae principia in quadam communmitate [The teacher, who explicitly has the whole knowledge of a thing, can more expiditiously lead someone to this knowledge than can someone who learns it inducing it from himself. The teacher can do this from the fact that he knows the principles of knowledge in a certain community of knowledge]" (*De Veritate*, 11, 2, ad 4). That is, the teacher, the one who has learned himself, who knows his "science" or discipline explicitly, can by this very means better lead the student to knowledge than the student could lead himself. And Aquinas held that it is better to be able to teach or pass on things that we have contemplated, that we have delighted in knowing, than simply to know them by ourselves.

There is a certain excitement about things seen and known. We want to pass what we have seen to others. Hence, "visio docentis magis consistit in transfusione scientiae rerum visarum quam in earum visione: unde visio docentis magis pertinet ad actionem quam ad contemplationem [The vision of the one teaching consists more in the infusion of knowledge of seen things than in the seeing of them: hence the vision of the one teaching pertains more to action than to contemplation]" (*De Veritate*, 11, 4, ad 3). That is, the vision of the one who teaches consists in infusing the knowledge of things known rather than in the vision itself. The vision of the one who teaches pertains to the active life rather than to the contemplative life, though both are needed. Thus, there is an excitement in simply knowing the truth, the knowledge of things. And this excitement flows over naturally into our social nature. We want to explain to others how we arrived at or came to know the things seen. We become active; we want to talk, instruct, help others see what we see.

How, in conclusion, will we know whether we are educated? Let me recount one final story. On his Grand Tour, James Boswell reached the court of Dresden. Boswell was twenty-four years old at the time. On October 7, 1764, he met Monsieur Vattel, who was at the time the Privy Councillor at Court and the author of a famous book in international law, *Principes du Droit des gens.* Vattel explained to Boswell that he composed his book on the law of nations while Saxony was in confusion and he expected "to lose all that he had." Just writing the book served to calm his mind. Boswell was then introduced to Madame Vattel. According to Boswell, who had an eye for such things, she was "a handsome young Polish lady." That evening the Vattel couple were going to dine with Count Schulenburg, the Danish envoy. They graciously invited Boswell to accompany them. Several other gentlemen were also present. During the evening, they dined, played whist, and chatted.

Boswell, who was himself quite precocious, complained to Vattel that he, Boswell, was "ill-educated and had but little knowledge." Vattel replied, "Excuse me, Sir, you are well educated." Boswell continued, "The Envoy did not let this pass; he looked at me as one looks at one whom he admires, without well knowing for what. Vattel and I talked of learning in general, of the late war in Germany, of fate and free will, or more properly the origin of evil. He was for the chain of being. I stood well against him."[11]

No doubt, Boswell, at twenty-four, had serious problems, as he frankly tells us, with personal morality. (The young Augustine would have had no problem in understanding him.) Boswell thought himself ill-educated with but little knowledge, and if we reflect on all that Boswell was later to learn from Samuel Johnson, we know that he was right. Yet, Count Schulenburg was also right. As he listened to Boswell and Vattel chat, as he reflected on the range of their conversation from current politics to metaphysics and theology, he was aware that this young Scot was curious about many things, from the mundane to the profound. Perhaps he did not yet possess Aquinas's *ordo disciplinae*, but he did display a genuine Socratic *eros* for knowledge.

Thus, while it is true that some few of us can learn something of the truth by ourselves, from reality itself, as Aquinas maintained, still the normal way—the best way—is to learn the truth from someone who knows, even from the few great minds that may not have existed in the time when we ourselves were alive. We can indeed be deceived by our professors and by our own passions; Boswell was therefore fortunate to have Johnson. Still, what is essential, what is basic, is our own wonder, our own *eros*, our own willingness to be taught and awareness of our desire to know *all that is*.

In his *Confessions*, Augustine tells of coming across, at age nineteen, the now lost "exhortation to philosophy," the *Hortensius* of Cicero. Wrote Augustine: "This book in truth changed my affections, and turned my prayers to Thyself, O Lord.... Worthless suddenly became every vain hope to me; and with an incredible warmth of heart, I yearned for an immortality of wisdom..." (III, 4).

In order for the student, the potential philosopher, to be provoked, he must first be teachable, eminently teachable like Augustine. But the teacher must himself know, must know the order of the discipline and its relation to other disciplines. Many confusing and irrelevant things must be sifted through, lest the task be loathsome and confusing. In the end, both teacher and student must be about the truth, about *that which is*, about what neither made but what both must discover in a community of learning that includes not just themselves but those who have lived before them. And there must be a vision and an *eros*, a sense that what is merely human or merely mortal is not enough for us. It is not that for which we are made.

The most intelligent of the angels fell, demonstrating that human will and not ignorance is the primary cause of evil. The drama of our learning *what is* is paralleled by the risk that we will choose ourselves over reality. This is a risk we cannot avoid taking. It is in the nature of things. For it is this risk that ultimately incites us to choose a life in which teaching and being teachable lead us to that vision of *what is*, a vision that only a few of our kind have achieved without having been taught.

INTERLUDE I

On the Fate of Academic Men

IN THE DENT 1957 enlarged edition of J. B. Morton's 1938 edition of *Hilaire Belloc: Stories, Essays, and Poems*, we find an excerpt from *The Path to Rome*, Belloc's account of his walk from Toul, France, to Rome in 1901. This edition identifies Belloc in the following manner: "Hilaire Belloc, born on 27th July 1870. Educated at The Oratory School, Edgbaston. After leaving school served as a driver in the 8th Regiment of French Artillery at Toul. Matriculated at Balliol College, Oxford, in January 1893 (Brackenbury History Scholar, and 1st Class in Honour History Schools in June 1895). Died in 1953." Between 1895 and 1953, nothing is mentioned. We find no reference to Belloc's stint in the House of Commons, nothing of his family, his sailing, his relationship with Chesterton, or his voluminous writings. To the British mind, perhaps, all that is important about a life is the date of birth, the date of death, and, in between, what schools were attended, what academic honors were received, and what regiment was served in, even if it was a foreign army's. Perhaps that is enough.

The eleven-page extract from *The Path to Rome* begins with Belloc, very hungry, having just scaled a crest of the mountains. He has managed to find an inn called "The Bear" in the town of Ulrichen. Therein he is met by a middle-aged lady, "one of the women whom God loves." Belloc addresses her in French. She answers him in a "rustic" version of the same tongue. She looks him in the eye as she speaks to him.

This straightforward, untroubled gaze incites Belloc to think about academics—not his favorite folk, to say the least. "Beware of shifty-eyed people," he begins. Their nervousness reveals a kind of "wickedness." There is no doubt what will become of the shifty-eyed. "Such people come to no good." Belloc then asks the most marvelous question (he is speaking to himself, one of his "Lector"–"Auctor" passages). "Why do the greatest personages stammer or have St. Vitus' dance, or jabber at lips, or hop in their walk, or have their heads screwed round, or tremble in the fingers, or go through life with great goggles like a motor car? Eh?"

We have all met the man with the goggles, the one with the hop in his walk, the one with his head screwed round. From such men we never get a straight answer. Belloc informs us why, but we are hardly prepared for the reason he gives. "It is the punishment of their *intellectual pride*, than which no sin is more offensive to the angels."

All of this began, recall, when Belloc met the lady with the clear gaze in the Bear Inn. Clearly, she was not infected with the disease Belloc describes. But who are these prideful ones? They are those men who do not notice all the wonder to be found about them, those human beings who seem to be nothing more than mind. And unless a man is more than a mind, his mind is quite a dangerous thing. The angels are pure spirits; we are the rational animals, body and soul.

Belloc describes the situation of the mind-only-gentleman in this fashion: "What! here are we with the jolly world of God all round us, able to sing, to draw, to paint, to hammer and build, to sail, to ride horses, to run, to leap; having for our splendid inheritance love in youth and memory in old age, and we are to take one miserable little faculty, our one-legged, knock-kneed, gimcrack, grumpy intellect, or analytical curiosity rather (a diseased appetite), and let it swell till it eats up every other function?"

What does the sane man do when this happens? He yells, "Away with such foolery."

Belloc himself, of course, thinks the world of God to be jolly: he sings, draws, paints, hammers, sails, rides horses, runs, and leaps. He has had love in youth and memory in old age. And he tells us it is a "splendid inheritance." Perhaps he is still a bit annoyed that he did not himself end up as a pedant, though this is hard to imagine. He knew the dangers of his own "grumpy intellect," for it could lead him to the very pride from which he was perhaps saved when he could not stay at Oxford.

The "Lector" wants to get on with the walk and quit these dreary philosophical musings. But the "Auctor" has a few more things to say. He repeats, "Away with such foolery." He decides to explain the problems we have with the pedants. They "lose all proportion." Worse, "they can never keep sane in a discussion." Belloc gives us an amusing example. The pedants "go wild on matters they are wholly unable to judge, such as Armenian Religion or the Politics of Paris or what not."

On the other hand, a man with a steady and balanced mind, with a clear gaze, only has three things to remember to keep him sane. These are: (1) "After all it is not my business"; (2) "Tut! tut! You don't say so!"; and (3) "Credo in Unum Deum, Patrem Omnipotentem, Factorem omnium visibilium et invisibilium." In these last words from the Creed, Belloc thinks, all the analytical powers of the pedants and the professors are but "dustheaps" by comparison.

Belloc then stops to add, as if it is preposterous, "I understand that they [the professors] need six months' holiday a year." If Belloc had his preference, he would give them "the whole twelve, and an extra day on leap years." For if they are on vacation all year long, they cannot do much damage.

The "Lector" is anxious to get back to the story of the woman in the inn. And Belloc is willing to return to her. In fact, he has never left her example in all his chiding of the prideful academics who need six months' vacation a year. The sin of pride reminds him of the Day of Judgment. "[On this day], St. Michael weighs souls in his scales, and the wicked are led off by the Devil with a great rope, as you may see them over the main porch of Notre Dame (I will heave a stone after them myself I hope), [but] all the souls of the pedants together will not weigh as heavy and sound as the one soul of this good woman at the inn."

I saw Notre Dame a couple of times, but never noticed above the main porch the Devil with a great rope leading startled pedants to their doom. But, of course, I did not know Belloc then.

Belloc finally sat down to eat. The good lady brought him food and wine. He found the wine good. However, the food had in it a "fearful herb," a spice or scent, "a nasty one." "One could taste nothing else, and it was revolting; but I ate it for her sake." After all, "We have for our splendid inheritance, love in youth and memory in old age."

These are just a few of the things that the biographical sketch of Belloc did not mention. They make it possible for us to say with him, "Credo in unum Deum, Patrem Omnipotentem, Factorem omnium visibilium et invisibilium," for these are the things that confound the pedants and cause us to look "to see the jolly world of God all about us."

CHAPTER 3

❦

Truth and the College of Your Choice

I

AMERICAN CARS often have on their rear windows stickers indicating the preferred college of the driver or the driver's family—Ohio State, DePauw, Fordham, Cal Berkeley, Texas Tech, Iowa. No doubt, these emblems are placed on the car as a badge of distinction, as if it made a radical difference whether you went to Furman, Reed College, or Texas A & M. I have yet to see a decal saying MIT Ph.D. Such types are too cool. But you do often see Georgetown Law or UVA Med School. I suppose it would be too much to find hidden symbolism in such signs. Still, sometimes words speak louder than actions.

On my father's car, we had "Santa Clara University." I guess it meant that the frequent driver of my father's car at the time was no mere high school dropout. But a university's name on a car window might mean only that the driver roots for the Notre Dame football team, not that he actually went there. The college name also implies that the school to which the driver goes, or went, had or has a claim on him. The education presented there must have something distinctive about it. In this Honda Civic or BMW XL 900, the sticker implies, is no ordinary sophomore, but a brainy dude who is attending school with the Minnesota Golden Gophers.

Since I never really stopped going to school after Santa Clara, or at least never stopped teaching in one, I am not a good judge of the sundry claims that the various universities have made for their own peculiar excellences. I am in fact skeptical about it all. Political correctness is pretty widespread. I think in general that you can get a terrible education in the best and most expensive universities and that in fact most students do; I think Allan Bloom was right. I likewise think that today some of the finest educations can be had at very small out-of-the-way places like Thomas Aquinas College in California, or the University of Dallas, or Wheaton College in Illinois, or the philosophy department at the University of Nebraska at Kearney. Moreover, if you are lucky you can get a very good education in the worst of schools. A lot depends on you and who you run into, something at which Plato hinted. It is even possible, indeed likely, that those who educate you in the truth may not be found in any university at all. Augustine found a book of Cicero in some out of the way place in Carthage, and he happened to hear Ambrose in a church in Milan.

We read the *Symposium* of Plato in one of my classes, a dialogue that is particularly relevant to my topic here. I think we have all been struck in the class by the fact that our souls must be involved in the education we receive—or better, in the one we allow ourselves to receive. And this involvement of our souls, of our very selves, is not just for its own sake. The souls of the worst, after all, are as "involved" as the souls of the best in their own education. We have a soul in the first place to know and choose what we are in the light of *what is*, in the light of truth.

Ultimately, we are in charge of ourselves, whether we be in the worst, in the middling, or in the best academies. This fact does not mean that teachers are irrelevant, but perhaps they are not as relevant as they might like to think. Plato believed that the final overthrow of Athens was caused by a very handsome, exceptionally intelligent, witty, and carousing young man who could, but would not, rule himself. After we take a good look at what is there, outside of ourselves, as Aristotle said, all education begins and ends in our souls, in our view of the highest things, and in the courage we have to pursue them. As Eric Voegelin remarked, speaking of Plato, "The true philosopher is the man who loves to look with admiration at the truth. The truth of things, however, is that which they are in themselves."

Plato thought, however, that very often what we choose to study or to take up as our career—what we choose to be our "lifestyle," as it is now put—is a function of the disorder of our lives. This disorder can take root when we are quite young, as Plato knew. This was why he paid so much attention to the conditions of education. He figured that we often chose business, poetry, politics, law, art, science, or even philosophy because we did not want to know or did not have the time, intelligence, or most often the will to learn the right order of things. In the seventh of his *Letters,* Plato advises us that the best way to find out if an intelligent young tyrant—all potential philosophers are also potential tyrants—was really interested in knowing the truth is to explain to him how much he has to sacrifice in terms of hours of work, singular devotion, poverty, and ridicule in order to be a true philosopher. Our universities, no doubt, are full of young men and women, potential philosophers all, who like the rich young man in the Gospels turn and go away sadly when they find what they must do to be good, to be perfect, to know the truth.

II

Once in a while, if one is foolish enough to ask, I will say to a student that it would embarrass me if he went through this (or any) university and did not carefully read Aristotle, not to mention St. Thomas. As a professor, I would be humiliated if one of my students found himself fifteen years from now—when he would be about the same age as the young man who betrayed Athens, Alcibiades, was in the *Symposium*— having to admit in a serious conversation that neither in his college years nor at any time since had he read anything of genuine importance. But the fact is that few opportunities exist for the careful reading of Aristotle or Saint Thomas, even if we should want to. A thousand other claims and requirements inevitably prevent most students from even thinking such a thing might be a good idea.

Moreover, no one can imagine how much it distresses me to realize that a student knows absolutely nothing about the Bible, as if this lack of knowledge will lead him to anything but hopeless floundering. After watching the last of "The Civil War" segments on TV, I asked my class why the freed blacks after the Battle of Richmond, crowding around President Lincoln, called him "Father Abraham." Not everyone knew. One very nice young woman, after having read a brief assigned text from the Gospel of Luke, asked me with some wonder if this was where the story of the Good Samaritan came from. I assured her that it was.

The philosopher-novelist Walker Percy wrote:

> The old modern age is ended. We live in a post-modern as well as a post-Christian age.... It is post-Christian in the sense that people no longer understand themselves, as they understood themselves for some fifteen hundred years, as ensouled creatures under God, born to trouble and whose salvation depends upon the entrance of God into history as Jesus Christ.
>
> It is post-modern because the Age of Enlightenment with its vision of man as a rational creature, naturally good and part of the cosmos which itself is understandable by natural science—this age has also ended. It ended with the catastrophes of the twentieth century.[1]

What age we begin in the twenty-first century is a question of some moment, especially if reason too, as Percy intimates, is ending. In this same essay, Percy amusingly reports that when asked why he is a Catholic, he retorts, "What else is there?" When spelled out, I suspect that Percy's answer is as profound as anything that has appeared on the subject in generations.[2]

And yet, in spite of my enthusiasm for Aristotle, Aquinas, and the Bible, I am not a big fan of courses in "the great books." For the most part these programs are heady substitutes for genuine philosophy and end in a kind of trendy relativism. In an essay that every student ought to read—I have a modest list of "ought-to-reads", if anyone is interested[3]—Professor Frederick Wilhelmsen wrote, "Aristotle insisted that philosophy is the highest instance of the life of leisure, but there is no leisure for boys and girls who are expected to gorge themselves on three thousand years of texts and then regurgitate them come examination day. To remember all the data, as suggested, leaves no time for judgment. Yet judgment, says St. Thomas, is the mark of the philosopher of being...."[4]

No doubt, we need to know dates and data, just to begin. I have had hundreds of students over the years who, I hope, will never forget when Cicero died, let alone what he held. Ultimately, however, as Professor Wilhelmsen remarked, we have to "talk" philosophy into existence, something that Plato taught in the first place. (Many people would in fact be quite surprised by what Plato has to say about the dangers of writing as compared to those of speaking.) Conversation requires a kind of academic and moral leisure that is practically nonexistent in any university of my acquaintance. It is true that we have to work to have leisure. But it is also true that until we recognize the limits of work, we will think that work is our human destiny. That's what the Marxists thought, and we know what happened to them.

To be sure, we think that everything we ourselves read is important, including our assignments. After all, the great cliché of modernity is captured in the question, "Who is to say what is important?" I suppose that no surer sign exists that a student will learn little of importance in his life than his articulation of this question as if it has the status of revelation. Plato held that we deal ourselves our own punishments. The cruelest punishment for not knowing is, and remains precisely, not knowing. The real punishment of hell, of which Plato also talks, is the consequence of allowing us the freedom to choose ourselves as if we were the center of the world. We are left with ourselves.

I have frequently said to students, who look quizzically at me as if they are not quite sure whether to believe their ears, that the most difficult political act they will ever make is accurately to name the regime in which they are living—or visiting, for that matter. This same principle can be even more difficult to apply to our university or to our own souls. It seems obvious to say that it takes a humble and brave man to describe himself correctly, as if anyone can do it at all and still bear his fate. Yet, this naming is what we must do if we are to live honorably.

The best "ideal" university, the best university in speech, is probably still, after Plato's, that found in John Henry Newman's *Idea of a University.* But unlike Newman's university, I believe that it is practically impossible to obtain an education in the highest things in most existing universities. I do not say that especially loudly, and it is not necessarily a cry of despair. But the first thing one must notice about today's schools, if he is to begin at all, is that students have little real confrontation with the highest things, including the truths of revelation.

Philosophy classes or literature classes or theology classes or science classes will not in themselves do. Curriculum reform or new tracts or diversity training are not the ultimate answer. A polity's education is almost invariably something modeled on the state of soul of those who compose it. And the state of soul of today's dons is often quite at variance, too often for the worse, with the not-too-exalted level of most nonacademic folks. I think that education in the higher things today is largely a matter of private enterprise. That was more or less the thesis of my *Another Sort of Learning,* and I see no reason to change that view.[5]

III

What does it mean to say that education in the higher things is largely a "private enterprise"? "Private" education seems like a contradiction in terms, unless we remember what Plato and Aristotle held about the location of truth. *Amicus Plato, Amicus Aristoteles, magis Amicus Veritas.* Truth is only found in the judgment of a living, thinking person. The academic Left has never liked private enterprise, of course, even when it comes to education. And as numerous studies have shown, this Left primarily holds the power in the universities today. But there are some guides to be found. Plato said that it is not enough to find a book in which the truth is written, because even the noblest books are but collections of words and letters that cannot defend themselves. So, he thought, we have to find a teacher that loves the truth and loves us enough to guide us to it so that we can see it for ourselves. Nonetheless, books can lead us to teachers who do not exist in our own time or place. We need not be wholly dependent on teachers who are still alive.

But perhaps we are getting ahead of ourselves. For doesn't spending so much effort in obtaining a genuine education distract us from more important things, like helping the poor? I have long been struck by what Mother Teresa said about those who are the real poor in our midst. "It is very painful to accept what is happening in Western countries: a child is destroyed by the fear of having too many children and having to feed it or to educate it. I think they are the poorest people in the world, who do an act like that."[6] I sometimes think that the most difficult thing in the world to bear is the moral pity of a good and lovely woman, one who understands, as Mother Teresa did so vividly, that "a child is a gift of God." But the poor cannot be helped unless we know what it is that causes wealth in the first place. Good will or bad ideology is not enough. And on this issue, I fear, most universities are long both on good will and bad ideology. Again we must look elsewhere. George Gilder is a good place to begin, as is Paul Johnson or Lord Bauer. I suspect that if we get it wrong on the question of wealth and poverty—which is, after all, Plato's question about property and discipline and ultimate purpose—we will get it wrong on most other things.

It used to be fashionable to say that "man is created to praise, reverence, and serve God and thereby to save his soul." I think this is still pretty good stuff. We can lose our souls even in the best of regimes, universities, or think tanks. Conversely, it is quite possible to save our souls in the worst places imaginable. This latter truth is why Solzhenitsyn remains so important to us. He reminds us that even people in concentration camps can discover their own souls and a way to the Lord.

In other words, it was worth Socrates' time to spend a good deal of effort on Alcibiades, the brilliant young man who would not pursue the highest things—not because he did not have the ability, nor because he did not have the highest of qualifications, but because, as he himself said, he could not resist the "cheers" of the crowd.

The first question remains that which Aristotle presented to us, in his laconic way, at the beginning of the *Ethics,* namely, where do we locate happiness? What is it that we are seeking to achieve with our particular lives, lives designed not just for the polity or for themselves, but for eternal life? "But is that something we do in the university?" we ask. In a way it is. We cannot forget that any faith or philosophy worth its salt claims truth—except academic and cultural relativism, the dominant ideology, which ironically claims itself to be true but not culturally determined.

"What else is there?" Walker Percy asked. I like this question, not just for its brashness or its rhetorical flourish, but also for its seriousness. The young Augustine is a hero of mine because, like Alcibiades, the brightest young man of his time, he tried everything. Unlike Alcibiades, though, Augustine was enough within the tradition of Plato to insist on asking himself whether anything he did or heard was really valid. Unlike Socrates or Aquinas, who tested everything in thought and found it wanting, Augustine really tried it out, only to find the same restlessness that Socrates found.

"What," it might be asked, "has all of this to do with the college of your choice?" Little, perhaps. In *De Magistro,* Augustine reflected on the highest things with a young potential philosopher who was, in fact, Augustine's own son, Adeodatus. This is what Augustine told him:

You desire to know now what it is we strive after or at least you want it to be mentioned. But I want you to believe that I wish neither to have occupied myself with quibbles in this discussion...nor to have labored for petty or unimportant ends. Still if I say that there is a blessed life, to which I desire that we may be led under God's guidance, that is, by truth itself through stages of a degree suited to our weak progress, I fear to appear laughable because I have set out on such a road by considering not the things in themselves which are signified, but signs. But be indulgent with this preparation, since it is not for amusement, but in order to exercise the strength and keenness of the mind by means of which we can not only bear the warmth and light of that region where the blessed life resides, but can also love the true.[7]

Augustine was aware that the pursuit of truth would, for the most part, appear to be "laughable," particularly that truth that caused a Walker Percy to ask, "What else is there?" But Percy's is a good question. You won't find it asked much in the universities, but still, ask it—no matter what college sticker you put on your car's rear window.

CHAPTER 4

%

On the Education of Young Men and Women

There are people who think that it is wonderful to have a mind that is quick, clever, ready to see pros and cons, eager to discuss, and to discuss anything, and who believe that such a mind is that to which university education must give scope—regardless of *what* is thought about, *what* is discussed, and *how important* the matter is.

— JACQUES MARITAIN, *Education at the Crossroads*

As an atheist, I preferred metaphysics because it is the supreme science, the ultimate crowning of reason. As a Catholic, I love it still more because it allows us to have access to theology, to realise the harmonious and fertile union of reason and faith. It was not enough for me to live, I wanted a reason for living and moral principles which were based on an absolutely certain knowledge.... Among all the sciences, it is metaphysics which, after all, seems to me best suited for a feminine mind with a gift for abstraction.

— RAÏSSA MARITAIN, *Raïssa's Journals*

I

JACQUES MARITAIN wrote one book (*Education at the Crossroads*) and several essays (collected in *The Education of Man*) on education.[1] He considered education to be an art, perhaps in its own way the finest of arts because its object, when perfected, was the most beautiful of all the earthly realities. The closest analogy to teaching, Maritain thought, was medicine.[2] Neither medicine nor education created its respective subject matter or what it was to be healthy or complete once it existed. Each sought to lead or guide a body or soul to what it ought to be when it functions normally. Once in its normal status, the healthy body or the healthy soul should be left alone to do those myriad things that healthy minds and bodies do. Given that the body was healthy, it—that is, the human incarnate person informing it—simply lived, did the things that healthy human beings do. When man, body and soul, was educated, he again simply lived, did the wondrous things free and healthy human beings can do or, more darkly, freely did the things they ought not to do. Knowledge per se, as Aristotle told us, does not automatically mean that we will be virtuous (*Ethics*, 1105b2).

Education prepares our innate faculties and capacities to do what they were made or created to do. Man does not cause or have control over what he is. What he is, is given to him by nature. Man does not make man to be man, Aristotle said, but he does make him to be *good* man. We may be astonished that such a being as ourselves exists in the first place, that we had nothing to do with the making of ourselves. The drama of human existence, however, has to do with what a man, among his fellows, does with his given existence, because he can both know and rule himself in a curious freedom that enables him also to reject and revolt against what he is. The human good *includes* the ability to choose the human good. The human being can choose not to be what it is designed to be. The risk of human existence is its capacity to reject human existence.

Maritain held that the teacher was indeed a cause in the education of youth, but an instrumental cause—necessary for the most part, to be sure, but not the principal cause of education. The student was the *principal* cause of his own education. Interestingly, Maritain showed a certain persistent, optimistic sympathy for students, not untypical, I suppose, of those who have no children of their own. He thought everyone could be educated in the important things, and not only that they could be but that they should be. And he was willing to admit only a small place in education for strict scholastic discipline. We have all heard the expression, "Spare the rod and spoil the child." Maritain evidently referred to this saying in his own attitude to physical discipline. "Education by the rod," he affirmed, "is positively bad education." He then added, amusingly, "if from a love of paradox I were to say something on its behalf, I should only observe that it [the rod] has been able, actually, to produce some strong personalities, because it is difficult to kill the principle of spontaneity in living beings, and because this principle occasionally develops more powerfully when it reacts and sometimes revolts against constraint, fear, and punishment than when everything is made easy, lenient, and psychotechnically compliant to it."[3] Maritain even wondered whether making things too easy for students did not produce indifference and passivity in them. But he was much more concerned about inspiration, play, and the delight of seeing things for one's self. Neither "birch and taws [floggings]" nor the teacher himself ought to be the principal agents in education, Maritain believed.

In *Education at the Crossroads*, Maritain cited the remark of Professor F. Clarke at the University of London to the effect that a certain "stringency and tension" were needed in education. Clarke added that "original sin may be more than an outworn theological dogma after all," that "of all the needs of democracy, some abiding sense of the reality of original sin may yet prove to be the greatest."[4] To this sober remark about the existential condition of the subject of education, Maritain immediately added that, as a Catholic, he agreed. Nonetheless, Maritain had one caution, namely, "that an abiding sense of the reality of the internal power of regenerating grace and faith, hope, and charity, may prove to be even more necessary."[5]

Maritain, in other words, was willing to talk about Christianity as if it were a legitimate topic of conversation and as if it had something both positive and necessary to contribute to our understanding of education. He did not, to be sure, want anyone to be forced to study theology in nondenominational schools, but he thought anyone without a knowledge of theology would simply not understand humanity and probably not himself. "Modern philosophy...has burdened itself all through modern times with problems and anxieties taken over from theology, so that the cultural event of philosophy purely philosophical is still to be waited for."[6] That is, all actual philosophy not only bears the mark of some theological consideration, but, to use Maritain's perceptive phrase, "philosophy purely philosophical" always reveals itself to be somehow incomplete, even for its own purposes.

II

I have entitled this chapter, "On the Education of Young Men and Women." Maritain, of course, spoke rather of the "education of man," using that word to mean, in context, any person, male or female, of a rational human nature. He did not make too much of the sexes' differing approaches to the highest things, such as we might find in Gertrude von le Fort's *Eternal Woman* or even in some of the writings by his own wife, Raïssa. However, we find one striking exception to this general approach, an exception that occasioned my reflections here. In 1941, George Schuster was inaugurated president of the then all-female Hunter College in New York, and Maritain was invited to give an address which he entitled, "The Education of Women."[7] This essay developed a thought that he had already got from his wife about the place of metaphysics in the education of young women.

To introduce this topic, however, let me begin with a classic text about the education of young men and young women. Charlie Brown is worried about his slow reading and is seeking an excuse that would not redound to his own unwillingness to work. He is hopeful that poor eyesight might absolve him. Linus, however, has been to the ophthal-mologist, who has explained to him the dubious relation between glasses and slow learning. Charlie, with some concern, asks Linus, "You say my being a slow reader is not caused by needing glasses?" Linus replies, "Prob-ably not." Linus continues authoritatively to a puzzled Charlie, "Slow reading in children is often the result of 'mixed brain dominance....' A person is right-handed because the left side of his brain is dominant...." In the third scene, Lucy appears from nowhere, intently listening as Linus proceeds, while Charlie hesitantly puts his hand on his chin, "Now if you are ambidextrous or if you have been forced to write with the wrong hand, this may produce 'mixed brain dominance....'" Linus concludes triumphantly to a bewildered Charlie, "If this is true, we can rule out poor vision as the cause of your slow reading." The last word, however, as we might expect, goes to the ever-logical Lucy, who asks Linus the really worrisome, unspoken question: "Have you ruled out stupidity?"[8]

In his various discussions about the education of young men and women, Maritain largely downplays both original sin and stupidity as major problems, or at least as insurmountable ones. For instance, he affirms that "in a social order fitted to the common dignity of man, college education should be given to all, so as to complete the preparation of the youth before he enters the state of manhood." I am not sure whether Maritain ever goes into the problem of obtaining financing, private or public, for such a system, but a bigger problem is his assumption that everyone should go to college. Not that he doesn't have some reservations about his own thesis. "Exacting from all pupils the same degree of rigorous study and progress in all items of the curriculum is most unwise." A natural "apathy" toward many studies will probably be normal.

What about the lazy student, someone we have all met at one time or another, perhaps in ourselves? "Laziness must be fought, of course, but encouraging and urging a youth on the way which he likes and in which he succeeds is much more important, providing, however, that he be also trained in the things for which he feels less inclination, and that he traverse the entire field of those human possibilities and achievements which compose liberal education."[9] Maritain's educational project, then, though formidable, is weighted on the side of learning because it is itself a delightful and worthy thing to do.

III

Maritain began his lecture at Hunter College in the midst of World War II by remarking that "culture today stands in need of defense."[10] For Maritain the word culture connoted wealth, technology, industry, and scientific equipment. But primarily it meant knowing "*how* and *why* to use these things for the good of the human being and the securing of his liberty." Culture is primarily inner formation. To develop inner strength is another way of talking about what the ancient writers called the virtues, both of mind and heart. The soul cannot be destroyed by force. "The soul yields only when it so wills. Culture implies the pursuit of human happiness, but requires also that we know in what this happiness consists." These are words directly from Aristotle and Aquinas. Culture includes the habits of our tradition. "Culture consists in knowing, but it does not consist only in knowing; it consists even more in *having known*, and in the forgetting of a great many things because we know them too well and because they have passed down from memory into the very marrow of our bones."[11] Included in culture is the liberty that the founders of the American Republic knew. If we do not know the reasons for living and for dying we will not keep our culture.

Maritain next acknowledged that not everything can be learned in books, but he insisted that books and lectures "are an indispensable and basic vehicle of what man should know, and that without schools worthy of the name, there is no culture." Maritain recalled Goethe to emphasize the priority of being over having, something John Paul II often emphasizes. Action follows being. Maritain suggested, carrying out the implications of this position, that the mission of the school respecting culture is greater in women's colleges than in men's, for women have more leisure for "being" than men do.[12] He called it their great "privilege and duty." Somewhat in the tradition of Tocqueville, he remarked that America is known for being a land favorable to youth and women. Since women are so important for culture, Maritain thought, the teaching of young women was "doubly important and significant."

Maritain, moreover, saw no truth in the idea that women did not possess the intelligence to attain the highest levels of excellence. He thought, however, that there was a welcome and necessary differentiation or complementarity between the sexes that was good for culture. "My already long experience as a professor has shown me," he continued,

> that often young women enter into the realm of knowledge with an intellectual passion more ardent and a love of truth more disinterested than young men do. If they are usually less gifted than men for the constructive synthesis and the inventive work of reason, they possess over them the advantage of a more vital and organic feeling for knowledge. When they love truth, it is in order to bring it down into life itself. When they love philosophy, it is because it helps them to discover themselves and the meaning of existence; and they well understand the saying of Plato, that we must philosophize with our whole soul.[13]

Young women have more need of unity, Maritain thought, the result of which meant that an overly departmentalized education was more damaging to women than to men. He cited his old teacher Henri Bergson, who did not think that women were in fact "more gentle and compassionate than men," and supposed Bergson was right in this, but Maritain did think women were "less naive and more courageous in the face of public opinion" than young men.

The complementarity of male and female was not seen as an opposition but as a necessity. Men had perhaps better judgment, women better intuition. The prodding and perception of women often disconcert, but without it human culture would lack its richness. To teach the same discipline to young men and to young women reveals often that "the same discipline is received in different ways," a result that is a source of richness for the culture.[14]

Raïssa Maritain's notion that metaphysics was a preferred study for women suggests the truth of Jacques Maritain's remarks about how differently and more ardently young women receive the same subject matter. "It was not enough for me to live," Raïssa Maritain wrote in 1919, "I wanted a reason for living and moral principles which were based on an absolutely certain knowledge." Very often, Maritain observed, young women may not realize the long historical and intellectual effort it took to bring "the human person, in woman as in man, to a consciousness of its dignity." Christianity played an original role in woman's emancipation when the Gospel was preached to Greek and barbarian, to male and female alike. Maritain can be blunt at times: "The sense of human dignity is the mark of every civilization of Christian origin and foundation, even when our fickleness of mind causes us to forget it."[15] Maritain saw that the political notion of human dignity followed from the Christian notion of each person's supernatural destiny, not vice versa. Even in the natural order, following Aristotle, there is something in each person that transcends the state:

> The human person, even though it be part of the political community, has within itself values and a calling which transcend the political community, for they are things that rise above time. Truth, beauty, wisdom are sovereignly useful for the State, they are not at the command of the State. The State must serve them, just as the State must respect in each one the fundamental rights of the person.[16]

Since there are things in the natural order that already transcend the state, the state is limited. All of these natural things are put into their proper place, however, only when the supernatural destiny of men is understood in the light of man's "philosophy purely philosophical."

Maritain ended his little essay on "The Education of Women," then, not with an exhortation to women in particular but to all those who would be educated, men and women. He calls what he stands for "a democratic education." This is "an education which helps human persons to shape themselves, judge by themselves, discipline themselves, to love and prize the high truths which are the very root and safeguard of their dignity, to respect in themselves and in others human nature and conscience, and to conquer themselves in order to win their liberty." If we reflect on this vision of education, does it not seem, in retrospect, that Maritain's project has largely failed, at least as an institutional project?

IV

Maritain's elaborate program for all levels of education endeavored to spell out the various stages of teaching according to the age and maturity of the student. He was also interested in graduate and postgraduate education. If we turn to the question of the education of young men, however, we will find very little written by Maritain specifically on this subject. What we do find, rather, is a detailed description of the person who is to be educated, almost as if to indicate that we cannot educate man unless we know what he is. I want to say something about Maritain's understanding of education from the perspective of his presentation of what the human (male or female) is who is capable of being the primary cause of his own education. And in conclusion, I will turn to Maritain's description of the famous "Thomist Circles" that lasted from 1919 to 1939 at Versailles or Meudon while Maritain was teaching at the Institut Catholique in Paris. I want to mention these groups because I think they represent something that is becoming increasingly necessary in the context of the modern university's political correctness, namely, an alternative to the university, not as a counter-institution, but as a human initiative that transcends the intellectual disorder now confronting us.

In his essay "The Christian Idea of Man and Its Influence on Education," as well as in some remarks he made on Plato and Descartes, Maritain took pains to set down the sort of being who was to be educated. He had earlier affirmed that "education is by nature a function of philosophy, of metaphysics."[17] This is no doubt one of the reasons that the penchant for metaphysics in the education of young women was so pronounced in the Maritains. If we do not know what or who it is to be educated, the whole effort will easily go awry. This understanding also hints at the importance of there being no philosophy that is itself "purely philosophical"; that is to say, the philosophic life, however valuable, cannot itself be identified with the happiness to which each human person is intrinsically ordained.

Maritain is quite willing to state the uniqueness of the Christian understanding of man. Not unlike John Paul II in *Crossing the Threshold of Hope* or Augustine in the *Confessions*, Maritain states clearly his understanding of competing views of man. Christianity, for instance, does not teach the "transmigration of souls," a view that implies that eventually each of us is everyone else, even every other thing. The Christian alternative is a version of the Greek philosophic idea of the immortality of the soul. "After the death of the body the human soul lives forever, keeping his own individuality."[18] But this understanding of immortality is not all. Faith holds that "the body will rise up and be united with the soul again." Even after death, the immortal soul is not in a state of completion, a completion that would necessitate both body and soul. Against Hinduism and Platonism, which hold the soul to be the essence of man, the Christian idea includes at all times the body, or the whole person as the completion that is really implied by man's standing as a being made for nothing less than God. Descartes's notion that the individual is essentially mind is likewise to be rejected as incomplete. This excursus into philosophy is important. A lofty understanding of man's soul at the expense of his body is not a Christian alternative. Christian philosophy grounds the whole educational enterprise by placing both body and soul in right perspective with regard to the final end of the whole person.

"Christian education does not worship the human body, as the ancient Greeks did," Maritain wrote, but it is fully aware of the importance of physical training as aiming at a sound balance of the whole human being; Christian education is intent on making sense-perception, which is the very basis of man's intellectual life, more and more alert, accurate, and integrated; it appeals confidently to the deep, living power of imagination and feeling as well as to the spiritual power of reason; it realizes that in the development of the child hand and mind must be at work together; it stresses the properly human dignity of manual activity.[19]

Maritain was careful to pay tribute to Plato while still making clear why a proper understanding of education did not follow from the notions of innate ideas or man-as-essentially-soul. Human souls do not preexist, nor are they replete with ideas the understanding of which is obscured by the body, so that the highest understanding can only be had if the body is removed. In the Platonic understanding, the pupil "does not acquire knowledge from the teacher, who has no real causal influence and who is at best only an occasional agent; the teacher only awakens the student to those things which he already knows, so that to know is nothing else than to remember."[20]

Maritain thought that this Platonic system treated the human being as if he were an "angel." He also noted that in the *Laws*, Plato, far from stressing this angelic knowledge, seemed to propose an extraordinarily detailed list of things to which the citizen had to conform, something that implied the lack of an active practical intellect responsible for judging the particular cases in which normal human life usually consisted. Maritain's alternative was that of Aristotle, which proposed a more realistic understanding of the relationship between teacher and pupil. "The teacher does possess a knowledge which the student does not have. He actually communicates knowledge to the student whose soul has *not* previously contemplated the divine Ideas before being united to his body; and whose intellect before being fecundated by sense-perception and sense-experience, is but a *tabula rasa*, as Aristotle put it."[21] It is of some importance to spell out this background understanding of what man is because it alone can justify the combination of man's physical and spiritual sides in one whole. Body and soul are essentially related to one another because of an end that itself transcends not only the state but also philosophy—without being hostile to either.

V

Maritain thought that there was an intimate relationship between the pursuit of truth, education, and the spiritual life. The higher the level of education the more deeply attentive we must be to things of the spirit, taken in the Christian sense of the incarnational unity and destiny of each person. Maritain, for all his praise of philosophy, did not think that by itself it would succeed in sustaining the idea of human dignity among men. "Thus we may understand the paradox that natural law exists, as the very basis of morality, and that nevertheless no effort of reason to establish among men a firm system of morality based only on natural law has ever been able to succeed...."[22] Some evidently paradoxical relationship exists between the supernatural and man's natural inability in this life, at least, to be natural. This paradox, this dilemma, helps explain Maritain's organization of the "Thomist Circles." He noted that throughout history—in India, China, Europe, among Quakers and Catholics—"wise men living in solitude and contemplation gather together disciples who come to listen to them either for a certain number of years or at certain times of the year."[23] Within the Catholic tradition, Maritain thought, the times especially required the formation of spiritual centers wherein spiritual life and instruction could be developed. This sort of experience would also be advisable for university students and boys and girls during school vacations.[24]

In his *Notebooks*, Maritain described his own experiment with this sort of program, one that combined study, prayer, conversation, and a sort of family environment. The Thomist Circles, as they were called, met once a month at the home of the Maritains. They were designed for "those men

and women for whom the spiritual life and studies in wisdom (philosophical and theological) had a major importance and who wished to
devote themselves as much as they could to pursuing them."[25] The formal
structure of these groups, its written constitution, is printed in the appendix of Maritain's *Notebooks*.[26] It even included a private vow of prayer
and devotion, though there was no idea of a religious congregation. The
people who attended are listed by Maritain as they appear in one or other
meeting. They were a "varied ensemble," including

> young persons and old persons, male students and female students,
> and professors—laymen (in the majority), priests and religious—
> professional philosophers, doctors, poets, musicians, men engaged in
> practical life, those who were learned and those who were unedu-
> cated—Catholics (in the majority), but also unbelievers, Jews, Ortho-
> dox, Protestants. Some were already experts in St. Thomas, others were
> serving their apprenticeship with him, others knew nothing about him
> or almost nothing.[27]

There was a climate of friendship and liberty. The atmosphere was not
that of class or convent or seminar, nor were they "guests of a more or less
stiff intellectual [figure] trying to offer them seats and passing out drinks
and cigarettes before the exchange of ideas." Rather, the success of these
afternoons and evenings was largely due to the presence of Maritain's wife.
"They were received in the hearth of a family, they were the guests of
Raïssa Maritain. Such meetings and such a work in common are inconceiv-
able without a feminine atmosphere," Maritain wrote. Not only Raïssa was
present but her sister Vera and her mother. Raïssa is described as present,
taking an active part in the discussion, "always discreetly, but with the
mad, boundless love of truth which burned in her." This peculiar phrase
"mad, boundless love" appears often in Maritain's notes almost by way of
challenge to those pedestrian souls who are not ready or willing to engage
in the real drama of human existence in the knowledge and love of God.

What was the subject matter of these circles? They always concerned some great theological or philosophical issue broached in a text of St. Thomas Aquinas or John of St. Thomas. "The fundamental idea was to bring into play at one and the same time, in the concrete problems and needs of our minds, things we knew to be diverse in essence but which we wanted to unify within us; reason and faith, philosophy and theology, metaphysics, poetry, politics, and the great rush of new knowledge and of new questions brought by modern culture."[28] Maritain himself prepared immediately before the meetings a brief exposition of the matter to be discussed. His notes contain outlines and sketches of what he had to say. He gives a list of the subject matters for the first ten years of the circles; they range from angelic knowledge to human knowledge of singulars, the desire for the vision of God, speculative and practical knowledge, justice and friendship, the Trinity, the person, the Incarnation, free will, and the analysis of the voluntary act.[29] There was a constant effort to clarify language, to appeal to direct experience, but a "fierce search for intellectual rigor." "The experience of our study meetings taught me a very precious thing," wrote Maritain,

> namely, that discursive and demonstrative argumentation, doctrinal erudition and historical erudition are assuredly necessary, but of little efficacy on human intellects such as God made them, and which first ask to *see*. In actual fact, a few fundamental intuitions, if they have one day sprung up in a mind, mark it forever (they are intemporal in themselves), and they suffice...to make a man unshakably strengthened in the love of St. Thomas and in the understanding of his wisdom. I observed this in a good number of our friends, whose example I take to be decisive.[30]

Maritain seems to imply that academic experience, at its highest level, requires spiritual vision. We must first ask to "see" before we shall see.

VI

Maritain's experience in the Thomist Circles seemed to confirm his experience in teaching young women as well. These students were unhappy because with the presuppositions of their philosophy, there was nothing left to see. Raïssa Maritain as a young woman loved metaphysics because it was "the ultimate crowning of reason." She loved it more because it gave her access to something higher, not higher than reason, but to a reason that is higher than *human* reason. Thus did Jacques Maritain conclude that the kind of education one received made a difference. What was really important was not one's quickness of wit or specialization of knowledge, but what one learned to think about and discuss.

That St. Thomas could guide us in sorting out things of importance to discuss, Maritain had no doubt. We can say without too much exaggeration that today graduates of most universities—public, Catholic, or private—have simply never had the things that really matter clearly and adequately explained to them. Yet the student has to desire to know, and he has to suspect, at least, that he is not really encountering the great questions—and what is more important, the great answers. When the Platonist tells us that our knowledge is innate, or when the Hindu tells us that we are already reincarnate, or the Cartesian that we are only mind, we must be ready to see something else. And there is an intrinsic relationship between the moral life and the intellectual life. When the habits of our human wholeness are not in order, we will not be likely to think straight. But our bodies can be perfectly healthy and we can will not to see.

A way of access to "a reason for living" is, among us, the most important of the things we can receive from education. We should not doubt that the original sin that Professor Clarke spoke of, or the stupidity that Lucy suspected, or the relativism that Allan Bloom observed the best students embracing uncomprehendingly, can deflect us. But even the most perceptive theoretical knowledge and education will little avail us as we actually are, as Maritain said in his *Notebooks*, unless, like Augustine, "we first ask to *see*." This seeing requires our first knowing what we are and, yes, praying for what we want to be. If we do not know some purpose for ourselves, we will not be able to fulfill that great Socratic admonition to "know ourselves," for we cannot know even ourselves by knowing *only* ourselves.

"The task of the teacher," as Maritain said in a final sentence that we can properly apply to Maritain himself, is not one of "birches and taws," but "above all one of liberation."[31] What really matters are the right answers to the right questions. The endeavor of the twenty-first century may well be that of finding new Thomist Circles, new families, new universities, new monasteries, perhaps even new technologies, wherein the right questions and the right answers can be asked and given. But what is important is not the technology that is used, but the seeing, the desire to see, the discipline and grace of life that enables us even to want to see.

Ch. 1

We tend to take what we consider the more "important" of our activities - generally work, as opposed to play - too seriously. Human affairs have their place and their seriousness, but there is a bigger picture that makes all those things seem rather unimportant when you see the whole. The so-called "frivolous" or "pointless" things in life are the ones that often lead us to understand God and the world best and lead us to contemplation.

Interlude IV

Self-discipline is important, but not in the way many view it. It is the beginning, not the end or goal. Once we have learned to control ourselves and order our lives we are freed up to pursue the important things in life that we would otherwise not have had the liberty to understand.

Ch. 3

The quality of your education does not hinge primarily on the prestige of the school you attend, but on your ability to get a good education yourself. Education deals not simply with reading the truth but with understanding the truth for yourself. Also, education is more than reading and knowing a lot of facts. You need time to examine and judge the things you read - to really think about them.

Ch. 2

A couple of things must happen for us to truly learn. First, we must have the desire, the "eros" for learning that drives us generally to want to know about things. It, then, is possible to learn without a teacher, but it is difficult and many are discouraged by the disorder of learning. It is better to discover the order of learning and pursue that.

Contemplata Tradere

CERTAIN QUESTIONS, good questions, never seem to be asked any more. Certain other questions, even when asked, confine the range of possible answers by some *a priori* theory or prejudice. Our character is decided too much by what we do not want to know, especially when what we do not want to know is in fact the truth.

When I am not busy writing law school recommendations for otherwise normal students, students who even seem to understand that about 70 percent of the world's abundant supply of lawyers already exists in the United States, I wonder if these students ever ask themselves about ends? I know the question of "ends" cannot safely be mentioned in the polity itself, because that would imply that some "lifestyles" are better than others. We do not want that sort of sentiment around. Virtue cannot be a viable option, for that would mean that some things are vices. Still, as an act of rebellion, it is good to wonder about things that we are not supposed to think about. Wonder, after all, is one of those things that most distinguish our lot, as Aristotle once said.

Thomas Aquinas inquired about which sort of religious life was best: one devoted to contemplation, one devoted to an active life like giving alms or attending the sick, or one in which elements of both contemplation and action were present. In giving his answer to this query, Aquinas used an example. "Just as it is greater to illuminate something than merely to shed light, so it is greater to pass on to others what we have contemplated, than just to contemplate" (ST, II-II, 188, 6). That is a neat image, I think—a light illuminating nothing.

Few would suspect that in that brief passage much controversy lies hidden. The first thing Aquinas suggests is that bishops are supposed both to teach and to contemplate. It is a good thing to imitate their examples. (We wonder whether Aquinas was not merely defining what bishops are supposed to do, but also urging them to do it, as if perhaps some don't.) It is not enough, moreover, to do good works or pray to God. What we do should directly flow from what we think and pray about. Behind Aquinas's brief remark is an awareness of the wholeness of our being, that we are to think and act—to think before we act, and to act on the basis of what we think. We are to contemplate, that is, think rightly about the *things that are.*

The early Jesuits, a couple of hundred years after Aquinas, came up with their own way of stating this truth. Their emphasis was not so much *contemplata tradere* ("to pass on to others the things contemplated") but to be, as they put it, *in actione contemplativus* ("contemplative in action"). *Contemplata tradere,* the Dominican formula, implied the noble task of spending much time figuring things out, then going forth to teach and preach what one had drawn into his soul. The Jesuit formula, for its part, suggested that what goes on in the world of action has its own spiritual content. We were to behold this content as it was made manifest in the visible world. One could interpret the Jesuit formula either as seeing the very newness of divine providence working itself out in the events of the day, or as being engaged in worldly affairs with a certain distance in order to realize the abiding things of God in all things—even in the events of the day. It is well to remember, though, that the Jesuits were also sup-posed to have read St. Thomas!

What does this reflection have to do with ends, virtue, and not adding to the world's supply of lawyers, with the questions that do not seem to be asked any more? We are to take into our souls *all the things that are*, even the meaning of our own actions. Those things that flow into us and those things that flow out of us belong to one world. We are not complete if we do not reflect on the highest things, or even on our own things. Nor are we complete if we do not seek to relate all things to one end, not just to any end, but to the truth of things.

We need not all be bishops, or Dominicans, or Jesuits, or professors, or lawyers, or aides in hospitals, or providers for the poor, though we can choose any with a good spirit. But in each of our actions, we are to behold not ourselves but the *things that are.* We are to pass on those truths we have first contemplated and reflected on. If no one teaches us this truth in our own world, we are to seek a world in which such things can be asked. We are not to be defeated by the questions no professor or politician will ask us.

In actione contemplativus. Contemplata tradere. In these two phrases, we can rediscover the world in all its causes.

CHAPTER 5

❧

On the Mystery of Teachers
I Never Met

Things are known in two ways; for some are known to us, some known unconditionally. Presumably, then, the origin we should begin from is what is known to us. This is why we need to have been brought up in fine habits, if we are to be adequate students of what is the fine and just, and of political questions generally. For the origin we begin from is the belief that something is true, and if this is apparent enough to us, we will not, at this stage, need the reason why it is true in addition; and if we have this good upbringing, we have the origins to begin from, or can easily acquire them. Someone who neither has them nor can acquire them should listen to Hesiod: "He who understands everything himself is best of all; he is noble also who listens to one who has spoken well; but he who neither understands in himself nor takes to heart what he hears from another is a useless man."

— ARISTOTLE, *Nicomachean Ethics*

I

In the *Apology*, Socrates brought up the question of whether he was paid for being a teacher, like the Sophists, who, when they came to town, were paid for their skill in teaching whatever it was that someone wanted to know. Socrates was dubious about the Sophistic claim to teach while, at the same time, being indifferent to the goodness or badness of what was taught. Socrates further maintained that he was not in fact a teacher, nor did he take any money for anything he said. If someone learned from him, it was only indirectly, by listening to his examination of those who claimed to know. And the imitation of his ways could be dangerous, as he found out when he was called before the court by fathers who were angry that their sons used Socrates' methods rather flippantly on their sires.

Properly speaking, then, teachers cannot be paid for what they teach. For what they teach, if it is true, is not theirs. They do not own it. They did not make it or make it to be true. This fact is why any financial arrangement with a true teacher (I do not mean here just anyone employed by a school system) is not a salary or a wage but an "honorarium," something offered merely to keep the teacher alive, not to "pay" him for ownership of a segment of "truth" said to be exclusively his. What he who teaches knows, then, is known for its own sake, not for his sake— even when the knowing is, as it should be, his. Truth is not like private property, something we should own and cherish. Rather it is something that, when passed from teacher to pupil, makes both something more and neither any less. Truth is of the spirit, the "conformity of mind and reality," as Aquinas said. The motivation of the teacher has to be something intrinsic, some "love of wisdom" for itself.

Besides, teachers do not need much in the way of material goods, as their delight is really not to be found in financial rewards; if a teacher does seek wealth, his teaching is suspect. This was, at least, the Socratic attitude toward the economic status of the philosopher. The reason the philosopher was not rich was not because he did not know how to become rich. The reason the philosopher was poor was because he knew that there was something beyond riches, something that carried a fascination little realized by those immersed in wealth, at least until they became old, when they might begin to worry about their death and, in its glaring light, about how they had lived. A teacher, rather, gives an account of truth—his account, but not his truth. "The origin we begin from," Aristotle said, "is the belief that something is true...." If we are brought up with fine habits, we can be "adequate students of what is fine and just." Someone else, however, brings us up. We are beholden to others not only for our very being but also for our good habits, if we have them. We are beholden to those who guided us so that we can easily see and, if we choose, arrive at the first principles on which all truth stands. Teachers and students are in the same condition with regard to truth—they stand before something neither the one nor the other made. The modern idea that the only truth is the "truth" we ourselves make is a narrow view that quickly cuts us off from *what is.*

A teacher is content to see the light in the eyes of the student who, after some guidance perhaps from parents the teacher does not know, some prodding, some examples, and some reflection, begins to see—and to delight—in the truth of things. The teacher must, at his core, be unselfish, must rejoice in what is not his. This is the liberty of truth that links generations and friends to each other.

The human spirit transcends time and space. And even if one of the great minds is not alive during our days, or if we are not lucky enough to meet such a person, we need not despair. We still can find the great thinkers, can meet them and let them teach us, through books. Indeed, with the new technology, it almost seems that no one is ever really dead. We can search for and find the works of someone who lived in the twelfth century—perhaps those of St. Bernard of Clairvaux—if we so choose.

II

I was once at Canisius College in Buffalo, where a fellow Jesuit showed me how to find on-line, from Carnegie Mellon University in Pittsburgh, the complete text of Chesterton's *Orthodoxy*, a book written in 1908. Suddenly, there it was, perhaps my favorite book, whole and entire, on the screen before my astonished eyes. But the technology used to put this text before my eyes, be it noted, is not more enchanting than Chesterton's thoughts themselves. What he said is, as it were, the miracle, not the technology that keeps it alive, though keeping it alive is one of the main functions of civilization itself. In the beginning, the words of what we now know as written Scripture were kept alive by oral recitation and memory. It is still in some sense the best way. We are what we choose to remember and to record. Yet, we can also forget our very being, if we so choose. Civilization does not depend so much on memory as the choice to remember, and on what we choose to remember.

Of course, I already have a couple of printed versions of that wonderful book I saw on the monitor in Buffalo; it is a book, in fact, primarily about gratitude, or better, about an understanding of the world in which gratitude is even possible. Chesterton, in his *Short History of England*, defined gratitude in a way that distinguishes our lot and, hopefully, our civilization. "I would maintain that thanks are the highest form of thought; and that gratitude is happiness doubled by wonder."[1] Why would Chesterton call thanks precisely "the highest form of *thought*"? I think it is because he understood that the world was not made by us. We can only give thanks for what we receive. And we can only give thanks to a some*one*, not to a some*thing*. Thanks are always addressed to another man. A world in which thanks for the world itself is possible is a world, a cosmos, in which the world is not sufficient to explain itself.

And gratitude—what about gratitude? Obviously, Chesterton thought it was something more than thanks, which he held to be the highest form of *thought*. He called gratitude "happiness doubled by wonder." And according to Aristotle, "wonder" is the source of our quest for knowledge—not need, not pleasure, not pain, but wonder, something on a much different and higher level. Happiness, that end that explains why we do all that we do, is "doubled" when we have a sense of wonder.

We are curious, as it were, that such things as the world and grateful-ness should exist at all. The initial wonder inaugurates the strange quest that sets us on the journey to find the truth of *what is*, of what is to be wondered at, since *what is* is not ours. And the doubling? First, we are the ones who give the thanks; indeed, this is our highest activity, as Plato would have said. But, second, we give thanks knowing that this act is appropriate and fitting. There is a some*one* to thank, hence the exhilaration.

It has been Chesterton, more than anyone else, who has taught me that it is quite all right to acknowledge that there are certain things that I will never do—which is another way of saying that "man is by nature a social and political animal." I need not myself discover the North Pole, a discovery Chesterton called "that insidious habit," nor need I be the Astronomer Royal, though I need not *not* admire those who do still find the North Pole or the North Star again and again. I can be grateful to them and admire them. But if I am going to do these sorts of things, I have to do them well, otherwise I shan't do them at all. And there are other things, fundamental things, that I want to do, even if I do them badly. "If a thing is worth doing," Chesterton said, "it's worth doing badly." In *What's Wrong with the World*, the example Chesterton used of a thing worth "doing badly" was dancing. In reciting Chesterton's apho-rism about "doing things badly," I have never had a class that did not immediately both laugh and also understand what he meant when danc-ing is used to illustrate the point.

In *Orthodoxy*, the examples Chesterton used to illustrate this same principle were "writing one's own love-letters or blowing one's own nose"—again examples that no one can fail to comprehend. Now Chesterton was not against the fine and noble practice of dancing well. He would have had, I am sure, no objection to Ginger Rogers and Fred Astaire or the Royal Ballet. But he realized that for most of the men and women who had ever lived, dancing badly was their only option if they were to dance at all. Many a touching love has been kindled, no doubt, while dancing badly, or at the instigation of awkward love letters.

Chesterton penned his aphorism some four years after my father's birth in 1904. My father, I believe, danced well, a talent that quite pleased the family. It was Chesterton who taught me the philosophic principle about dancing badly. But without my father, I would never have understood the importance of dancing well. As another friend carefully explained to me, on hearing Chesterton's principle, things that are worth doing are also worth doing exceedingly well, including dancing. But to do most things well, we must begin by doing them badly. There is no other way. Without my father I would not have known the importance of dancing well. Without Chesterton, I would never have understood the importance of dancing badly. I knew my father. I did not know Chesterton.

III

Augustine died in A.D. 430. On his feast day (August 28), I reread in my breviary the Second Lesson from the *Confessions.* "Urged to reflect upon myself, I entered under your guidance into the innermost depth of my soul. I was able to do so because *you were my helper.* On entering into myself I saw, as it were with the eye of the soul, what was beyond the eye of the soul, beyond my spirit: your immutable light."[2] Is there anyone today who tells me to "reflect upon myself"? And if so, do they instruct me to do it with divine guidance? Is there anyone who tells me that when I reflect on myself, it is not myself that I discover, that I am not the end even of my own desiring, of my own self-reflecting? The "immutable light" is not myself. And for this, too, I give thanks and double thanks.

When the philosopher in the cave, in the Seventh Book of the *Republic*, was unchained, turned about, and allowed to leave, he was eventually blinded by the light, the light in which he saw the truth of things. There are teachers like Plato and Augustine who still teach us that the truth of things transcends us. We have heard it said that the light shines and the darkness comprehends it not. Those who teach us about this light mostly do not come from our time or place. They do not usually speak our language. If it is all right to dance badly, because dance we should, it is all right to reflect on ourselves badly, in the depth of our souls, because the "immutable light" is not just for the philosophers. Indeed, this is why Thomas Aquinas maintained that philosophy, good as it is, is not enough, because the immutable light is supposed to shine also on the non-philosophers, even on sinners.

One of the teachers of whom I speak, Charlie Brown, can still be encountered rather regularly, as can that great theologian of the Fall, Lucy Van Pelt.[3] In one cartoon, Charlie is on the mound yelling to the outfield, "All right team, this is our last game of the season! Let's all do our best!" We next see Lucy in her baseball cap out in right field, yelling back provocatively, "What if we do our worst?" Charlie, somewhat perturbed, snaps back, "You've already done your worst!" And with surprising humility, Lucy admits, "I can't argue with that...." It is indeed hard to argue that we have not done "our worst" as a response to encouragement to do "our best." We cannot dispute the fact that doing our best and our worst are both possibilities for us. This is not to say that, having done our worst, we have no evil things left to do, but it does recall the Fall, *Genesis's* teaching about why things go wrong, and it calls us to the honesty to admit that they do go wrong—and that we have done something that caused the wrong to happen.

IV

Flannery O'Connor died of lupus in 1964 in Georgia. I never met her, heard of her, or even read anything by her while she was alive. But some friends from Athens drove me into the yard of her farm, Andalusia, outside Milledgeville one Sunday afternoon about twenty years after she died. Flannery O'Connor wrote to Cecil Dawkins on December 9, 1958, that she had broken her rib coughing and advised Dawkins that if she ever got a cough to buy some cough syrup in time. Evidently, Dawkins had, in a previous letter, asked O'Connor something about the Church having too many sinners in it for her comfort. Flannery replied that she did not want to be too glib in responding to such a query, but she would offer her "perspective" on the topic.

"All your dissatisfaction with the Church seems to me to come from an incomplete understanding of sin," Flannery told Dawkins.

> This will perhaps surprise you because you are very conscious of the sins of Catholics; however what you seem actually to demand is that the Church put the kingdom of heaven on earth right here now, that the Holy Ghost be translated at once into all flesh. The Holy Spirit very rarely shows Himself on the surface of anything. You are asking that man return at once to the state God created him in; you are leaving out the terrible radical human pride that causes death. Christ was crucified on earth and the Church is crucified in time, and the Church is crucified by all of us, by her members most particularly because she is a Church of sinners. Christ never said that the Church would be operated in a sinless or intelligent way, but that it would not teach error.[4]

Thus, in a way, did Flannery agree with Charlie Brown: the worst had already happened and continues to happen. Lucy is never going to catch the fly ball on the last game of the season. Pride, "terrible radical human pride," is always going to be with us, in part because we underestimate sin, in part because we are free and fallen. Because of these two things—pride and freedom—the world is at risk, a risk without which there would be neither happiness nor damnation, without which there could not be a finite rational being at all.

To want to have the perfect game, to want to have the Holy Ghost come along and transform all flesh into the Kingdom of God on earth, is therefore to ask that we live in another kind of world from the one we are given. It is implicitly to ask that we cease being what we are. Yet things worth doing are going to continue to be done badly—by human beings, by believers, even by clerics, all of whom are sinners. And unlike many modern-day liberals, no real Christian, nor anyone else who really thinks about such things, wants to change human nature, which is created good and continues to be good in spite of the Fall. Though any true Christian wants to stop sinning, this is something that can only be done freely. The liberal mind, however, desires the Kingdom of God on earth to be constructed as soon as possible and furthermore views this project as one to be brought about by our own powers and according to our own image of what is good. Augustine said that we *find* "immutable light"; we do not *cause* it to be either light or immutable.

Blaise Pascal was born on June 19, 1623. The second century Roman emperor Marcus Aurelius wrote a most memorable book called, simply, *Meditations.* I wrote a book, following Marcus Aurelius, called *Unexpected Meditations Late in the XXth Century.*[5] The Roman emperor taught me, not exactly to meditate, but to see things, to observe carefully, and to note what it is that things cause in us. Pascal's book—I believe he did not really finish it—is called simply "Thoughts"—though we still prefer the French *Pensées.* His book is very much like that of Marcus Aurelius's in form. We cannot resist the irony of an emperor "meditating," while a Christian apologist has "thoughts." Number 847 of Pascal's *Pensées* reads: "If the compassion of God is so great that He instructs us to our benefit, even when He hides Himself, what light ought we not to expect from Him when He reveals Himself?" What "light" ought we not expect? Of course, as Augustine would say, "the immutable light" is what we will find, even though we can in no way "expect" it.

The mystery of teachers we have not met, I think, lies here in these relationships and overtones. The gratitude to which we testify seems to have no limits because we are all bound together in time. We can still feel the force of those we never met, often because someone else felt it before us. The verb "to read," especially in British English, can mean "to study," "to learn from." Augustine explains that he once read a now lost dialogue of Cicero, the *Hortensius,* and it changed his life, a life that needed changing, to be sure. I explain to my students that Aristotle had read Plato. I explain that Augustine knew Plato. I tell them that Augustine read Cicero, who sent his son to study in Athens so he too could read Plato. Thomas Aquinas read Aristotle carefully. Pascal knew his Augustine. Even Charlie Brown knows that the worst has already happened, while Flannery O'Connor, who read Aquinas, recalls The Fall and our "terrible radical human pride."

V

In 1906, Hilaire Belloc published a set of essays he called *Hills and the Sea*.[6] We are with Belloc as he crosses the Channel in his small boat. We walk with him into the Pyrenees. We muse with him about great inns—like "The Griffin"—which may have never existed. We are with him at Carcassonne and Lyon. We see the Valley of the Rother as he does. We know his horse "Monster." We march with French troops. We go to Andorra, to Ely, and to Arles. One of his essays is entitled "The Idea of a Pilgrimage." The pilgrimage, of course, is the symbol of our lot. We are wayfarers and pilgrims on this earth, as Scripture reminds us. But it is a real earth, a real lot, a real way.

Belloc explained the outlook of the man who goes on pilgrimage. The true pilgrim will go "into everything with curiosity and pleasure, and be a brother to the streets and trees and to all the new world he finds," Belloc wrote.

> The Alps that he sees with his eyes will be as much more than the names he reads about, the Florence of his desires as much more than the Florence of sickly drawing rooms; as beauty loved is more than beauty heard of, or as our own taste, smell, hearing, touch and sight are more than the vague relations of others. Nor does religion exercise in our common life any function more temporarily valuable than this, that it makes us be sure at least of realities, and look very much askance at philosophies and imaginaries and academic whimsies.[7]

Beauty loved is more than beauty heard of? Why would Belloc say this? Clearly, in these observations, Belloc is telling us not only to read about things but to know them, experience them, even desire them. Christianity is a very earthy thing, after all. It encourages taste, smell, touch, hearing, and sight. Only if we know what these things are will we suspect the reality they imply as their source, "the immutable light." Each existing thing is a word made flesh, as it were. How odd it is to hear Belloc say that the most important function that religion can perform in time is to make us sure of "realities," as if our philosophies are often mostly imaginary abstractions.

VI

I read something from Boswell's *Life of Johnson* almost every day. I am familiar with the Mitre Tavern and St. Paul's, with Litchfield and Oxford. I know Lucy Porter and Mrs. Williams and the handsome Quaker lady, Mrs. Knowles. I am aware of the tension that exists with Mrs. Boswell. There is in Boswell an unending account of human life, its intense delight and poignant sadness. I have never quite forgotten the Journey to the Western Isles that Boswell and Johnson took in 1773; even now, I cannot come across the name of the Isle of Skye and not want to go there—but I want to go there for Belloc's reasons, for the sight, the sounds, the touch, the smells. Neither Boswell nor Johnson would have disagreed with Belloc's principle about how to see while on pilgrimages. Indeed, Belloc had no doubt read both Boswell and Johnson. Chesterton, for his part, wrote essays on both Boswell and Johnson.

Johnson was never a teacher, that is, an academic. (Neither was Socrates, Christ, or Chesterton, for that matter). What is it about Johnson, I frequently wonder? What is it that Boswell sees? The day is a Friday. It is April 20, 1781. David Garrick, the great actor and their mutual friend, has died. His widow has been in mourning, but the period is over. This evening was the first time since her husband's death—which, Boswell notes, she seems to have truly felt—that Mrs. Garrick has had a select party of her husband's friends dine with her. Boswell was there, of course, as were Dr. Johnson, Miss Hannah More, "who lived with her [Mrs.

Garrick] and whom she called her Chaplain," Mrs. Boscawen, Mrs. Elizabeth Carter, Sir Joshua Reynolds, and Dr. Burney.

Of this particular evening—all good things happen in a particular time, in a particular place—Boswell said, "I spent with him [Johnson] one of the happiest days that I remember to have enjoyed in the whole course of my life." They dined, of course. "We found ourselves very elegantly entertained in her house in the Adelphi." They spoke of her grief, but without morbidity. "She talked of her husband with complacency." She remarked poignantly that "death was now the most agreeable object to her." A painting of Garrick was on the wall, on which Johnson's friend Mr. Beauclerk had once inscribed in honor of Garrick the lines from Shakespeare that began, "A merrier man, / Within the limit of becoming mirth, / I never spent an hour's talk withal. / His eye begets occasion for his wit...."

We might, on reading Boswell's comment that this was one of the happiest days of his life, wonder about the appropriateness of the sentiment. And yet, as we read on, we realize that here we hear spoken of the ultimate, the fine, and the ordinary things of our human lot. "We were all in fine spirits," Boswell continued, for the death of their friend was now put into place in their lives, its mystery accepted. Boswell next turned to Mrs. Boscawen and whispered, "I believe this is as much as can be made of life." Boswell concluded his description of this happy day in this surprising manner: "In addition to a splendid entertainment, we were regaled with Litchfield ale, which had a peculiar appropriated value. Sir Joshua, and Dr. Burney, and I, drank cordially of it to Dr. Johnson's health; and though he would not join us, he as cordially answered, 'Gentlemen, I wish you all as well as you do me.'"[8]

Was Boswell wrong that no more can be made of life? Ought we be perturbed that on this happy day, a widow spoke complacently of her late husband, the actor, a merry man? Ought we be scandalized by the Litchfield ale with its "peculiar appropriated value"? No, I think here Boswell is right. He had sensed civilization at its best, where elegant things are served and the ends of life and transcendence have their place in the delight and joy we are allotted in this vale of tears.

On the 700th anniversary of the death of Thomas Aquinas, along with other members of the faculty of the Gregorian University in Rome (where I was teaching at the time) I got into a bus at the Piazza della Pilotta. We drove south along the main highway towards Naples. We came near Arpinum, the home of Cicero. Not far away was Monte Cassino, where St. Benedict founded the first monastery in the West, a commanding hillside now containing the tombs of Polish soldiers from World War II. Across the valley from Monte Cassino, where Thomas had himself begun school, was the little fortress town of Roccasecca, where Aquinas was born. There was a Mass, a goodly crowd, and I thought of the man. I remember vividly the day at Mt. St. Michael's College in Spokane when I first realized that I could read and understand Aquinas in Latin, that I did not have to "translate" him. St. Thomas's Latin, of course, is neat, simple, and clear.

Question Forty-Eight of the Third Book of Thomas Aquinas's *Summa Contra Gentiles* is entitled, "Quod Ultima Hominis Felicitas Non Sit in Hac Vita." This sentence simply is the proposition to be proved, namely, that man's ultimate happiness is not found in this life. It is what, with numerous arguments, Aquinas intends to demonstrate, and it must be read in light of Boswell's happy day spent with friends at the Adelphi:

> Quanto aliquid est magis desideratum et dilectum, tanta eius amissio maiorem dolorem vel tristitiam affert. Felicitas autem maxime desideratur et amatur. Maxime igitur eius amissio tristitiam habet. Sed si sit in hac vita ultima felicitas, certum est quod amitteretur, saltem per mortem. Et non est certum utrum duratura sit usque at mortem: cum cuilibet homini possibile sit in hac vita accidere morbos quibus totaliter ad operatione virtutis impeditur, sicut phrenesim et alios huiusmodi, quibus impeditur rationis usus. Semper igitur talis felicitas habebit tristitiam naturaliter annexam. Non erit igitur perfecta felicitas.

[The more something is desirable and loveable, so much more will its loss bring greater grief and sadness. The greatest happiness, however, is desired and loved. Its loss, therefore, will have the greatest sadness. But if the highest happiness were in this life, it is certain that it would be lost, at least by death. And it is not certain that it would last even to death since it is possible that there happen, to any sort of man in this life, sicknesses which completely impede the function of his reason, such as madness and other sorts of disease by which the use of reason is impeded. Such a happiness will have sadness naturally connected with it. Therefore, there will not be perfect happiness in this life.]

Notice how Aquinas and Boswell occupy the same universe; they use the same discourse of happiness, of happy days, of what this life is like and what it is not like. The essential issue is not, though, whether we can have a happy day, with some excellent Litchfield ale, toasting Dr. Johnson. The issue is the status of this happy day—without denying that it *is* happy, or, as Boswell whispered to Mrs. Boscawen, that "this is as much as can be made of life." It is indeed. Our happiest day, however, is not just itself but is also a promise and symbol. It will not, in all probability, be lasting. But the tradition that we inherit does not deny that we shall have happiness, perfect happiness, even double happiness. And this teaching remains true even when, trying to do our best, we have already done our worst.

VII

In *Another Sort of Learning*, I have provided a number of what I consider useful book lists on various topics or by various authors, things that most of us would not come across unless someone told us of them. In it, I list fourteen books by Josef Pieper, who is, not unlike Thomas Aquinas about whom he wrote so much, perhaps the most clear and concise writer on philosophical things I have ever read. Pieper died in 1998. I never met him.

In *Another Sort of Learning* I also listed twenty-five books labeled

"Schall's Unlikely List of Books to Keep Sane By—Selected for Those to Whom Making Sense Is a Prior Consideration, but a Minority Opinion." On this list there are two books by Pieper: *In Tune with the World: A Theory of Festivity* and *The End of Time*. Another book, Pieper's *Anthology*, is a book of selections that Pieper chose himself, and in this book of things to be read there are many beautiful chapters. One is called, "Joy Is a By-Product." The subject of joy, of course, touches the highest reaches of our being. But it is not something that we can go out and pursue. It never comes that way. It is always, as Pieper points out, a by-product. It comes from doing something else, from doing what is right and good. What is the nature of joy then? The common denominator of joyous experiences is, Pieper observes, "our receiving or possessing something we love—even though this receiving or possession may only be hoped for as a future good or remembered as something already past. Consequently, one who loves nothing and no one cannot rejoice, no matter how desperately he wishes to...."[9]

How do we love? What is love? These are commonly perplexing questions, but they are of ultimate import, since we are constantly faced with them in the risk of daily life. It is Pieper who, for me, identified in a graphic way the relationship between love and joy. Pieper says—shockingly but truly—that "the true antithesis of love is not hate, but despairing indifference, the feeling that nothing is important."[10] For those who are alive, for those who are attentive to the tastes, smells, sights, and sounds of the world, and for those who are alive to one another, everything is important because *it is*. We will not find complete happiness or the immutable light in this life, as Aquinas and Augustine warned us. But we find real things, finite things, that do exist. We experience, like Boswell, days that do not get any better. Their very completeness is a sign of their leading us on to what is complete, to what is joy, to possessing what we love. This too is our tradition. This too is taught by someone I never met.

A book that has gone through more printings and translations than almost any other, besides the Bible, is *The Imitation of Christ*, written by the fifteenth-century monk Thomas à Kempis. A friend of mine once found in a used bookstore a copy of some sermons that Thomas à Kempis gave to the novices of his order at Mt. St. Agnes. These sermons cover the various virtues and vices of monastic, or indeed of any human, life. At the end of each sermon, à Kempis adds a homely example to illustrate his point. One of the sermons, the sixth, is entitled, "On the Night Watches against the Assault of Sleepiness," concerning the Divine Office the monks sing each day. Writes à Kempis: "A certain brother began to sleep a little at Matins (the early morning part of the Office). Noticing which, the brother seated next to him cast into his ear just this word: 'Hell!' On hearing this, suddenly terrified and awakened, he cast off all drowsiness from him. Think therefore, slothful one, of hell, and thou wilt not slumber in choir, tired through weariness."[11] Hell or its equivalent is, in fact, found in much of our great literature and philosophy. It is, in part, the subject of the last book of the *Republic*. It is a book of Dante's *Divine Comedy*. It is a prominent factor in the *Brothers Karamazov*. But it is not talked about today. Is it because we too, like the monk, are drowsy? Is it that we too think nothing is really important?

Recall what Pieper said about the opposite of love being not hatred but "despairing indifference." Usually, and not unjustly, we associate the notion of Hell with hatred, but it is a hatred combined with indifference toward others. Indeed, Hell has been defined as a choice to love ourselves alone, closely associated with Flannery O'Connor's "terrible sin" of pride. We can have no love if we are ruled by pride. The doctrine of Hell has political implications as well. The second American president said that it was the most politically important of the theological doctrines. With Plato, John Adams knew that there are crimes that cannot be adequately known about or punished by existing polities, and therefore Hell renders justice complete.

Without a doctrine of Hell, furthermore, our individual actions have no real risk and no real meaning. If there is nothing that we can do that results in such a dire possibility, then nothing we do is really of much importance. On the hypothesis that there is no ultimate sanction, to do evil and to do well have the same effects and the same meaning. I have always, thanks to John Adams, Plato, and Dante, looked upon the doctrine of Hell as the guarantee of the importance of each of our actions.[12] It is not that we should not do frivolous things. There is indeed, as Boswell hinted, a certain lightsomeness to our condition. But it is a fact that at any moment we can be, and often are, faced with a choice that involves ultimate consequences because of the very exalted status of each person we meet, no matter how simple or how poor or how tiny. In a sense, the doctrine of Hell is the most romantic of teachings because it confirms what we already suspect: that our loves touch eternity and touch it because of the fact that something, some*one* is important, transcendently important.

VIII

Socrates, as I said in the beginning, maintained that he was not himself a teacher. But we know of Socrates because of another man, Plato, who was a teacher. In the *Crito*, Socrates testified that he was brought up by the laws of Athens. In the *Apology*, though, he states that his vocation to be a philosopher came from outside Athens, from the Oracle at Delphi who said that he was the wisest man in Greece. This unexpected information set him to inquiring about Athens to see who was wise. But though Socrates would not admit that he was a teacher, there is one passage in which he admits that he was taught. This is the famous scene in the *Symposium* with Diotima, the prophetess from Mantinea. Diotima taught Socrates about love, something that he evidently needed to learn from someone else, perhaps because love always has to do with someone else and not only with ourselves.

"Then," she said, "the simple truth is, that men love the good?" "Yes," I said. "To which must be added that they love the possession of the good?" "Yes, that must be added." "And not only the possession, but the everlasting possession of the good?" "That must be added too...."

"Then if this be the nature of love, can you tell me further," she said, "what is the manner of the pursuit? what are they doing who show all this eagerness and heat which is called love? and what is the object which they have in view? Answer me." "Nay, Diotima," I replied, "if I had known, I should not have wondered at your wisdom, neither should I have come to learn from you about this very matter." "Well," she said, "I will teach you: The object which they have in view is birth in beauty, whether of body or soul.... All men are bringing it [beauty] to birth in their bodies and in their souls" (206).

I began to read the *Symposium* rather late in my life. I met Adeimantus and Glaucon long before I met Phaedrus, Agathon, Alcibiades, and Diotima. To be sure, I had previously met Alcibiades in Thucydides. Likewise, I was introduced to Phaedrus, the master of ceremonies at the Symposium, some years ago, thanks again to Josef Pieper.[13] I have often told drowsy students, moreover, that the uncanny thing about Plato and Aristotle, about Aquinas and Augustine, is that they still make the best reading those students will ever encounter. I tell them—solemnly, provocatively—that if they do not read them, little else will be intelligible to them. For we cannot understand the romance of revelation if we do not understand the romance of reason, and there are some, I know, who want—that is, who choose—to understand neither romance.

Aristotle pointed out in the Sixth Book of the *Ethics* that we are given a mind as part of our constitutive being, a mind not given in vain. This mind is capable of knowing all things, it is *capax universi*, as E. F. Schumacher recalled in a wonderful book entitled *A Guide for the Perplexed*, a title taken from the medieval Jewish philosopher Moses Maimonides, who, like Avicenna and Thomas Aquinas, had carefully read Aristotle.[14] We find ourselves wondering about things *that are* on our walks with Belloc, in our conversations with Samuel Johnson, in our thoughts and meditations with Pascal and Marcus Aurelius. It is indeed mysterious that we can still be taught by those whom we have never met, that there can be a connection of mind to mind that leads to the good that we desire and which, when possessed, gives us joy.

We can indeed reject all the things about which we can wonder. We can refuse to acknowledge *what is* because it is not *of* us. The fact that we can do such things is the other side of the risk of existence, the fact that thanks can be withheld even from *what is.* But the risk of existence also includes, besides that which the monk whispered into his drowsy friend's at Mt. St. Agnes, the "immutable light." Boswell was able to sense that perhaps it did not get any better than his dinner at Mrs. Garrick's because he was in the sober presence of mourning; that is, he was prevented from seeking the Kingdom of God on this earth, a seeking which Thomas Aquinas and Flannery O'Connor warned us against. Man is fallen. Even Charlie Brown tells us that we have already done our worst.

In the end, Aristotle was right when he said that "who understands everything himself is best of all." Chesterton too was right when he affirmed that "thanks are the highest form of thought and gratitude is happiness doubled by wonder." None of these teachers have I ever met. The mystery is how one person whom I never met, through the filter of many others whom I also have never met, could shed light on each other, eventually to enlighten me. Surely this mystery has its origin in Augustine's "immutable light," in the Good which, when possessed, gives us joy.

INTERLUDE III

Order

St. Thomas often cites the famous phrase *sapientis est ordinare*—the function of the wise man is to order. We human beings have the added burden, if I can call it that—for it is also a glory—of ordering ourselves. To order ourselves means to properly place ourselves amidst the other things, including human things, that are not ourselves.

We human beings have a certain nobility. We can even protest what we are. We can think that it is unjust that we are what we are or that we are in the existential situation in which we find ourselves. Our defiance of what we are is not merely a statement of fact. It bears the mark of a positive opposition, as if we are talking to someone.

But we protest too much. We want God to make us free, but God has said that the only way we can be free is to know the truth. And we can choose not to know the truth. How seldom do we reflect on this enormous power. I like to think that God, when He created us, took the risk of God; that is, He could have chosen not to create us. It was not necessary for God to create, nor to create precisely us. We underestimate the Godhead if we suppose that God did not know what human choice entailed. It entailed the fact that we could choose to reject God and claim virtue for doing so.

St. Augustine explained that peace was the "tranquility of order." He knew the ambiguities of the word *pax*; imposed order can be a devastation, and even ruin has some sort of order. But the order from which tranquility stems is not that which comes from destruction. Nor does order mean absorbing all the constituent parts of a whole into a unity or sameness. Rather it means allowing the parts to function as parts, yet parts that are complete and not intended to be other than they are. Thus, when we die we are not absorbed into God. God keeps us as we are: finite human beings, indeed, particular human beings, each like unto nothing ever known before and nothing ever to be known again. We remain, we abide.

The scandal of the Incarnation is not that man is absorbed into God, but that the Word was made flesh and dwelt among us. God has His own internal order, which is revealed to us as the Trinity. And what is not God has its own order, which is essentially related to the inner life of God. We are promised precisely "eternal life," the life of God as our own end. Everything in us and about us is ordained to our achieving this end. We cannot, and do not, rest in what is not God. We cannot find anything that does not originate in God. Each tiny thing that we encounter, especially each human person, is directly related to the Godhead in all its glory.

C. S. Lewis remarked that we have never met a mere mortal. Our lives are not insignificant. They are risks. We really *can* lose our souls. Augustine thought that most people probably in fact did lose them. We like to be optimistic and suggest that no one loses his soul. But if this is so, it is hard to see how anything is of much importance. If nothing we do, say, or believe can really make any difference, what is our dignity? We may do what we want with impunity. Surely this is not the order of God for our good.

In God's intention, creation did not come first, then men. Men came first, then creation. We should not allow the size of space or its age to lessen the grandeur of spirit. We are given dominion over creation. We are to order it for our ends without denying what it is. Yet God does not "need" us. It is not that God was once unhappy but then found us. God was always happy, complete. But He took what I have called the risk of God, and so the order of our being is greater than we could propose for ourselves. This is why it is not ours to establish in the first place. *Sapientis est ordinare.* The end of all things is not that we establish here a lasting city. The end of all things is that, having been first chosen, we still must choose—choose not ourselves, but eternal life.

CHAPTER 6

❧

On Intellectual Poverty

The style of dress or manner of living in which anyone follows the faith that leads to God does not matter to the heavenly city, so long as these are not in contradiction with the divine precepts. Thus, even philosophers, when they become Christians, are not required to change their style of dress or eating customs, which do not impede religion, though they are required to change their false teachings.... With respect to those three kinds of life, the leisurely (contemplative), the active, and the combination of the two, although every one, through sound faith, can lead his life according to any one of them and attain the everlasting reward, what one holds through the love of truth and what one expends through the duty of charity are nevertheless important. Thus, no one ought to be so leisurely that he does not, in his leisure, consider the advantage of his neighbor; neither should anyone be so active that he does not consider the contemplation of God to be necessary.

— St. Augustine, *The City of God*

I

MOTHER TERESA OF CALCUTTA once remarked that the really poor people in the world are not those materially deprived in the Third World. Rather, they are the denizens of the intellectual classes in the affluent West who do not choose to know the truth and who do not want to know or abide by any norms—even divine ones—that they do not establish themselves. The implication of Mother Teresa's remark is, clearly, that things worse than physical poverty exist. "Seek ye first the Kingdom of God and all these things will be added unto you" is the Scriptural statement of this truth. Disordered minds are more troubling than disordered bodies, even to themselves. Modernity, in its extreme, wants to have "all these things" and call them, contrary to the Scriptural admonition, the "Kingdom of God." We will not be free, however, unless we also know the truth: the truth about ourselves and the truth about God.

Poverty, in fact, may protect us from many of the vices to which the rich in particular are susceptible. We cannot simply identify material prosperity with moral virtue; the one is not necessarily a sign of the other. History's greatest criminals and most corrupt villains have, for the most part, been rich, not poor. I do not mean to deny that certain rich men and women have been saints and martyrs, nor that many poor folk have seriously sinned and abused the rich (though more often the poor themselves).

Poverty does not immediately result in virtue. The Gospel is to be preached to all, rich and poor alike, not just to one *or* the other, and its reception is possible no matter what economic condition one finds oneself in. Scripture, in fact, only deals directly with this world insofar as it relates to eternal life. We are to look primarily to experience and the philosophers for how to organize this life in its practical details. The New Testament does not parallel Aristotle's *Politics* or the *Federalist Papers.*

Aristotle said, quite wisely, that most people probably need a certain minimal amount of material goods to be virtuous. But he was aware of the classical tradition that the philosopher should not much concern himself with riches even if he could have them. Aristotle even recounted a famous tale of how a philosopher, Thales, could become rich on the basis of his knowledge if he wanted to—by the age-old method of establishing a monopoly, it turns out. The philosopher preferred not to be bothered by the many obligations caused by the care of vast amounts of material things. This care would consume too much of his already limited time, which he thought better spent on the pursuit of truth.

To classical thinkers like Plato and Aristotle, the most important things were not economic ones, nor were they political ones—though engagement with both was natural and necessary, in proper proportion, for a full human life. The best things in life were, precisely, free. And it was not freedom that made us free, but truth. Paradoxically, the elevation of political or economic things to the center of human attention—one of the great temptations of the contemporary religious mind—corrupts not only the higher things, but also economic and political things by causing us to expect something from them that they cannot yield. Many a poor man has been told by intellectuals that what he needed most was riches, only to find out, on receiving them, that he was still empty. Modernity advised us to lower our sights from contemplation and virtue, to identify our happiness with the possession of its material substrate and not with the highest things themselves. We live in a culture dominated by a lower vision.

Dostoyevsky held that men would, in the end, choose to live by bread alone—and be told by their intellectual superiors that this bread is all there is, all there can be. Concern for religious and philosophical things was said to deflect us from the really serious things of this world. Plato said, however, in a remarkable and prophetic phrase, that the worst position in which any human being could find himself would be for him "to hold a lie in his soul" about reality, about *what is,* especially about himself, about what *he* is. To hold a lie in one's soul meant precisely to lie to oneself about what are the most important things, including one's place in reality. And this sort of distortion, we know, is the essence of heresy.

II

A commonly used phrase, one that the Holy Father himself often employs, though with considerable nuance, is the "preferential option for the poor." This phrase is designed not only to call our attention to the plight of the poor, but also to instigate action toward relieving their needs. The Jerusalem disciples, to recall, asked Paul to be "mindful of the poor," which he said he was glad to be. But Paul also worked so he would not be a burden. He warned those who would not work that they would not eat. The "preferential option for the poor" should not reduce the poor solely to objects of our exalted care, particularly bureaucratic care, with no input of their own into their own lives. The purpose of the poor is not to provide the state or the wise with a visible justification for their own activities, institutions, or experimental ideas.

This admonition to exercise a preferential option for the poor is primarily directed to our wills and feelings. Will and feeling can cause us to look elsewhere when we walk by a contemporary poor man. But we can also have a very earnest desire to "opt" for the poor without knowing exactly, or even vaguely, what we should do to make things better. In fact, many deeds and noble sounding programs, ostensibly directed to aid the poor, have actually harmed them. We are not wholly innocent when this unfortunate result derives from our best laid proposals. Many a well-intentioned idea or concern has turned out to be lethal in practice. We are quite familiar with efforts to alleviate poverty by providing abortions so that the "poor" would not come to be in the first place, so they would not "suffer" poverty. The really poor are, in fact, those politicians and intellectuals who propose such solutions.

In other words, no proportion may exist between our intentions and our deeds. Aid to the poor, no matter how well intentioned, does them no good if designed or implemented without sound intelligence, and quite frequently makes their lot worse. The purpose of "opting for the poor" is not to make everyone poor, even though certain believers can choose to be voluntarily poor to witness to some human purpose that transcends this world. Some grandiose plans to aid the poor—we think of the history of Marxism—not only end up making everyone poor, but also make everyone prisoners in an absolute state.

Most serious people thus recognize that ways offered to help the poor can themselves be either immoral or unworkable. Whatever the romance of Robin Hood, the fanciful method of stealing from the rich to give to the poor is basically wrong. Likewise, we have seen vast governmental sums poured into what is designed to be "aid for the poor," the whole superstructure of the welfare state, only to see it work to destroy families and to create a dependency and poverty far worse than what it was designed to alleviate. The twentieth century has shown, by contrast, that totalitarian regimes can, for a long time, feed and clothe the poor, which only teaches in yet another way that there are worse things than poverty.

In today's ideologically charged political atmosphere, we must be careful to distinguish between the subjective claim to choose for the poor and the effectiveness of the program that is proposed to implement this choice. Almost every ideology in the last three centuries was proposed as the best way to aid the poor, however these latter were defined. Indeed, the "aiding of the poor" often became a substitute for God as the only worthwhile end for a mankind that had rejected any transcendent purpose in its being. As God allegedly grew more and more obscure, the poor, usually taken as a mass abstraction, became the most "realistic" human purpose that existed outside the self-centered human person. The abstract poor served to give a touch of nobility to a world deprived of transcendent meaning.

III

Now, I do think that the poor can be "opted" for, but only if we keep a clear distinction between the classical ideas of charity and justice, only if we keep in mind a principle of subsidiarity that insists that the poor be largely helped to help themselves, and not be seen merely as objects of some all-caring state or state institution's pity, a pity that justifies everything in their name. Ironically, we are often very close to reducing all our social thinking to "charity," in which we conceive the people to be helped to be themselves helpless but for our own concern. "Bureaucratized social programs," Jennifer Roback Morse has written, "are no substitutes for the giving from one person to another that is the true meaning of *caritas*. And the modern state, which leads us to believe that there are shortcuts, that we can have the results of charity without the personal reality of charity, deceives us. Or perhaps I should say, we use the instruments of the modern state to deceive ourselves on these vital matters."[1] There is a common "guilt" that places the condition of the poor entirely in the hands of the state or the rich, as if that were sufficient. This move thereby gives to the state an identifiable social, even transcendent, purpose, but leaves the poor as merely the objects of someone *else's* benevolence or philanthropy. The Good Samaritan in the New Testament did not keep the man who fell among robbers forever dependent on him so that he could boast of his good deed. Rather he saw to his being taken care of so that he could soon return to his work.

But my topic here is "intellectual poverty." In recent years, our universities have often been structured so that students could be directed to various programs in the city or overseas wherein they could learn, first-hand but still vicariously, what it was like to be poor. This awareness of dire poverty was designed to waken the consciences of economically privi-leged students so that they would not merely desire wealth as their sole end in life and learning how to achieve it as their sole purpose in the university. We might call this the "service-oriented university." Behind this "service" concept, however, is often found an implicit picture of the world, sometimes marxist or socialist, often liberal and anti-religious, frequently heavily tinctured by environmental and anti-population ide-ologies. The poor really need none of these things.

Service-oriented programs have most often, in practice, been directed by and allied with what might be called the "intelligentsia university." It is quite clear that universities, almost of their very nature, are enclaves of privilege and leisure. They are designed in principle to be havens whereby the relatively young can be protected for a time from the pressures of life, of making a living, so that they can at least become aware of the higher things. The "service-oriented university" is often a thin veil worn by a kind of activist anti-intellectualism.

The purpose of the university is not, principally, the directing of students to the alleviation of economic or political problems, however noble this purpose might be, should something be found that works to that end. Indeed, if such a service- or business-orientation is the concept that a university has of itself, it will not do what it is designed to do with regard to the highest things, including the things of wisdom and God. Nor, it is my contention here, will such a university really do much for the poor. Before we ask about the ways to opt for the poor, we must deal directly with what we are, what are our relations to God, neighbor, and the world itself.

Mother Teresa's admonition is to be taken seriously. The affluent generally are the poorest of the poor, the most lacking in what is most important for human reality, beginning with truth itself. If we lack truth, especially if we deny that truth is possible—the relativist position that dominates almost every university faculty today—nothing else that we lack will really matter much. Truth is not the same as—though it is not necessarily opposed to—knowing a lot of useful things. But the wealth of the world consists in knowledge, a spiritual power and its activity, along with the virtue that incites its proper use. Moreover, the principal object of our knowing faculties is not the devising of means to alleviate poverty. Before we can think of the poor, we must first think of *what is,* of reality. It is a crime against humanity to make the materially poor also spiritually poor, to give them hope of only bread rather than every word that comes from God.

We do not live in a world that lacks ideas on how to help the poor. Indeed, we live in a world with thousands of programs intended to help the poor, though some never work. But we seem helpless to eradicate our intellectual poverty. We are told on a daily basis that there is a radical separation between our private moral lives and our public lives. We can be successful in public life, it is said, but have a moral life that radically deviates from the Commandments, which are said to have no basis in scientific reality. We are secretly comforted when public figures display vices that we would like to engage in ourselves. The great source of public immorality is always private immorality, or to put it differently, there is no such thing as a sin that does not have public consequences, no such thing as a sin that does not require repentance and hence acknowledgment of the intrinsic disorder it puts into the world. Intellectual poverty is rooted in, and tends to, moral poverty, to an unwillingness to know the truth in action, to recognize the distinction of right and wrong and, more importantly, to live it.

IV

The notion of intellectual poverty does not connote a lack of native intelligence or material goods. But intellectual poverty is indeed a lack of something—a lack of truth, particularly what John Paul II has often called "the whole truth about man." What intellectual poverty connotes is a refusal to ask the fundamental questions of life—about creation, death, freedom, sin, redemption, virtue—together with an unwillingness to listen to the answers, including the revelational answers, to these questions. The problem is not just an unwillingness to ask about such things but in not taking them seriously as vital constituents of our actual living.

And yet, we must wonder, granting that men are what they are—i.e., question-forming beings—why is asking such questions avoided? Are there things we don't want to know but suspect we can know? Do we avoid them because it would require a change in how we live? Here I am going to elaborate on something I learned from Aristotle, namely, that all intellectual errors are rooted in moral choices, in moral fault. This does not mean that morally good men cannot have erroneous speculative positions. But it does caution us not to take at face value any intellectual position that, in its logic, justifies a deviant moral position. Our model here is, no doubt, Augustine, who went through one intellectual position after another in order to justify a way of living that he knew he could not defend. It is amazing, even amusing, to note how furiously modern thinkers and politicians seek reasons to justify their deviant ways.

How does this justification work? The philosopher George Steiner, in his *Real Presences*, observes that one of the reasons that many Jewish thinkers lapse into ideology, into a search for a substitute messiah, is because it has, by their lights, taken so long for the messianic promise to be fulfilled. Eric Voegelin made a similar comment with regard to Christians, who also lapse into ideology because of their impatience with the delay in the Second Coming, however it is understood. We notice something similar in the Chinese, in their almost absurd borrowing from Marx to modernize their Middle Kingdom. But all of these aberrations suggest a common theme, namely, that an improper understanding of man's final destiny necessarily, yet still voluntarily, sets one off to find or create more rapidly the Kingdom of God on earth. This search justifies activities that violate the Commandments and reason in the name of a greater, more urgent good. I consider utopians of every sort, therefore, to be intellectually poor, however sophisticated their systems. They are modern Pelagians who do not see any need of grace, who do not see any need of an independent truth by which they might correct their ideas about what the world should be like. And behind all these lofty theories is almost always a sinful, deviant heart bent on rejecting that conversion of soul from which all social reform ultimately derives.

John XXIII was famous for many things, but one of the most important of his insights—one of particular pertinence today—was his explicit rejection of a radical split between private and public morality. He did not, of course, intend to deny St. Thomas's position that the state cannot command by its laws levels of virtue higher than the generality of men could be expected to observe. But he did intend to relate private to public virtue. "The same natural law, which governs relations between individual human beings, must also regulate the relations of political communities with one another," John XXIII wrote in *Pacem in Terris* (#80–81). "The individual representatives of political communities cannot put aside their personal dignity while they are acting in the name and interest of their countries; and they cannot therefore violate the very law of nature by which they are bound, which is itself the moral law." The idea of two different and separate moralities, one private and one public, a thesis stemming at least from Machiavelli, ends by corrupting both private and public morality.

Intellectual poverty is precisely the mind deprived of truth, of knowledge of itself and of the reaches of its thoughts and actions. The first step in this deliberate choice not to know the first things occurs when the mind rejects a standard in reality other than itself. It looks on its own spiritual life as self-constructed, self-composed. It cannot "do" any wrong, for it defines to itself what is wrong. Likewise, it cannot forgive or be forgiven because that would imply a source and measure outside itself. Intellectual poverty is the real origin of material poverty. This is why classical wisdom has always told us first to look to ourselves, to order ourselves by a standard that we do not create. When we choose an end that is deviant or corrupting, all the rest of our acts are chosen and directed to this end. Our minds work overtime to distort reality to fit our choices.

The most urgent need today is not attention to material poverty. The real poverty in our society is intellectual. Students attend universities, listen to professors, and come away intellectually poor, even when the university buildings and grounds are well ordered and charming. Thus, the alleviation of intellectual poverty is not something that can be solved with more money or new buildings. It is something that requires a transformation in the soul. As Socrates often told the young men who questioned him, they must "turn" and see something that they were not noticing because of the disorder in their own souls. When we choose to justify ways of life that deviate from the good, our intellectual lives are nothing less than sophisticated efforts to blind us from seeing *what is*. This is the history of our times.

CHAPTER 7

✾

On Wasting the Best Years
of Our Lives

I

Sally and Charlie Brown are standing by a telephone pole waiting for the school bus. Charlie is gazing down the empty street, while in back of him we hear Sally exclaim, "Someday there's going to be a monument here, and you know what will be on it?" Charlie continues looking down the street in silence. Sally continues to explain. It will read, "This is where Sally Brown wasted the best years of her life waiting for the school bus...." Charlie turns around to look at her with considerable perplexity as she describes what she would proceed to do with the wasted time. She would have "slept another ten minutes."[1]

Clearly Sally did not think that sleeping another ten minutes each school day morning would have constituted a waste of her time. The question of whether sleeping or waiting for school buses constitutes "wasting our time," however, is one of considerable interest if we think about human priorities. After all, we can only "waste" time if it makes a difference what we do or do not do with the time we have. If human lives and deeds make no difference to anyone or to anything, if life has no meaning, then all time is in vain, whatever we do.

One day I was walking off the campus when one of those huge garbage trucks came rumbling by. For some reason I looked at the truck rather carefully, and I noticed that this large-scale industry does not describe itself, in Washington at least, as in the business of "garbage collecting." Rather, it calls itself "waste management." But if waste can be so dignified that it can be "managed," then perhaps it is not, properly speaking, "waste" any more.

It is interesting to compare the usage of the word "waste" in these two contexts. Sally Brown "wastes" the best years of her young life waiting for the school bus. What is "wasted" is evidently time itself, as if there is some precious thing to do with time that is interfered with if we are just standing around waiting. We could at least be studying or, like Sally, simply sleeping. Evidently, both study and sleep have a purpose, while time wasted does not.

On the other hand, "waste" materials are no longer called garbage or refuse but precisely "waste." This "waste" is not collected and disposed of but managed, as if it had some proper order in itself. "Waste" is what no one needs, what is thrown away. We talk of "waste" land or "waste" paper. "Waste" has to be gotten rid of.

There exist various schemes to deal with the mountains of waste produced in any given city, schemes which see this waste as a potential source of heat, metals, building materials, or sundry other useful things. I once knew a dentist who invested in an invention to turn garbage into heat. Waste is on its way to becoming a natural resource.

I have read of some cities that make small mountains out of waste, on which they ski in the winter. Waste is not wasted. Indeed, it is doubtful whether anything can really be wasted; all waste has some use. It is mainly a question of knowing what a thing is and its alternatives. Poverty used to be a question of not having things. More and more, it is a question of not having brains or the discipline or freedom to use them.

Most "waste," I suspect, is a product of changing our minds or desires, which is quite a different kind of issue when we think about it.

The second-hand store or the second-hand book or the second-hand car exist because of changed opinions and changed tastes. Indeed, I think, the second-hand market is one of the great inventions of capitalism. Most of the housing market is composed of houses someone else has already lived in.

But there is still another use of this word "waste." In the famous book of Saint-Exupéry, *The Little Prince,* there is a wonderful sentence that reads, "It is only the time we 'waste' with our friends that counts." The point is very different, isn't it? Someone who is busy, occupied with many projects and duties is not likely to be our friend because he cannot spend time with us. He chooses to spend his time on "important" things, not us. But the Little Prince's point was precisely that in the highest things there was some conflict between daily duties and the deeds of friendship. For the former could interfere with the latter, however necessary the daily round might be.

To waste our time with our friends means that we do not have some sort of tight agenda, that we are not always looking at our watches or worrying about our lives. We need that very thing Sally was wasting waiting for the school bus. We need time. We need time-out-of-time, the time that passes without our noticing.

And perhaps we need also some openness to what might be called "waste," to the myriad topics and places that we are not curious about, yet which are there. Someone needs to protect us from the urgency of immediate things. We need a kind of escape from what everyone takes to be our main tasks. Perhaps there is something to be said not merely for wasting time but also for just waiting. Some things can be had too soon, when we are not ready for them.

Without too much scandal, it might even be possible to suggest that prayer is a kind of "wasting time" with God. After all, in prayer we do not really add anything to God. The only thing we can give Him that He does not already have is our love and our obedience. We are told, of course, to ask for certain things, "our daily bread," even that mountains might be moved. We are told not to worry too much even about what we wear but to look at the lilies of the field, that not even Solomon in all his glory was arrayed as one of these. Yet human raiment too is to imitate this beauty in a way. We are curious creatures who can add to our beauty and natural givenness. There is a kind of playfulness in God's dealings and admonitions with us, a kind of premonition of eternity in which time fuses into a kind of now, a presence.

On Tuesday, April 23, 1773, Samuel Johnson and James Boswell were conversing with a number of their friends, including Oliver Goldsmith and Sir Joshua Reynolds, on the reputation of the acting profession. Sir Joshua affirmed, "I do not perceive why the profession of a player should be despised; for the great and ultimate end of all the employments of mankind is to produce amusement."[2] Could Sir Joshua have been jesting? What's this "amusement" as the "great and ultimate end of all the employments of mankind"?

It is to be recalled, at this point, that Plato excluded all actors from his Republic on the grounds that they were twice removed from reality and taught us to be concerned with mere imitations of things. Thus, we will perhaps hesitate to affirm that the ultimate and great end of all the employments of mankind is to produce "amusement." Aristotle said that every activity we have is accompanied by its own pleasure and that this proper pleasure is a sign of the act's completion, of its being good. So was Sir Joshua's "amusement" a kind of delight or pleasure that served as a sign of our doing the right things at the right times and places?

No less a philosopher than Josef Pieper has beautifully argued that joy is indeed the end of all our longings and what is promised to us. So if there is but a short distance from amusement to joy, we can perhaps accept Sir Joshua's remark with rather more force than we might at first be inclined to do. We might not wince at all if we were to read, "The great and ultimate end of all the employments of mankind is to produce joy." And we might say this remembering that we are made in the image of God and that it certainly is proper to say that "the great and ultimate reality of God is joy."

Of joy, St. Thomas says simply, "Tantum gaudeatur de ea quantum est dignum de ea gauderi. Et sic solum Dei gaudium est plenum de seipso, quia gaudium Dei est infinitum, et hoc est condignum infinitae bonitati Dei [We should be joyful about those things in so far as they are worthy to be rejoiced in. Thus only God is complete joy in Himself, because the joy of God is infinite, and this is fitting to the infinite goodness of God]" (ST, II-II, 28, 3). If joy is proper to God, it must be proper to His creatures. Perhaps the words joy and delight and amusement indicate differing degrees of the same thing, proportioned to the different levels of being that we find in ourselves, in the world, and in God.

We now have, in any case, another word to put beside the concept of "wasting" time: "amusement." To be amused is one of the prerogatives of mankind. We are the only beings who laugh. Indeed, as Chesterton said at the end of *Orthodoxy*, the only thing that Christ did not reveal to us was precisely his "mirth." We are not told that God is not happy or joyful. Yet perhaps, Chesterton implied, we could not understand or even bear the sort of joy that was proper to God as reflected in Christ. It is something that we must wait for. St. Paul intimates that we cannot now imagine the joy that God has in store for us. We see but darkly. We know we live in a Valley of Tears. Yet in wasted time, in amusement, in laughter, we find breaking into our lives intimations that perhaps the sadness we experience is deceptive, however genuine it may be. The Liturgy even calls the Cross a *felix culpa*.

II

I heard on the radio one day an advertisement for a travel agency. I do not recall its exact name, but it was something like the Leisure Travel Agency. Here are two other words I wish to reflect upon: "leisure" and "travel." Is there any point in their association?

In the New Testament, we are called wayfarers and pilgrims. We are but travelers, as if to say that this is not our home. Someone who is only a traveler is a rather pathetic character. The man without a country is condemned to go from place to place without rest. But travel also implies a kind of freedom, an opportunity to satisfy our curiosity about other times, places, and peoples. The well-traveled man has seen the world, its different customs, languages, wonders. Like Herodotus, he brings back tales and accounts of his travels. But if he is perceptive, he will see that beneath the different cultural conventions, there seem to recur the same joys and sorrows, the same evils and amusements. It takes time to sort it all out, but though there appear to be vastly different ways to live a human life, this diversity is not so great after all.

Leisure is the noblest name of all. We have come to use it for the unimportant or superfluous things, or for the retired life. "Leisure villages" usually imply complexes composed of people who have retired from business and activity. The word "leisure" itself comes from the Greek word *skole,* from which we get the word school. And yet, few of us would probably describe what we do in school as "leisure." On the other hand, it seems odd that such great thinkers as Plato and Aristotle would associate leisure with the end of all we do, that they would hold that leisure is that for which we do everything else. But this is what they in fact claim.

Indeed, to understand what the Greek thinkers were getting at, we perhaps need to take another look at some of the words we have been using. Take again the word "amusement." As I said, this word bears the connotation of something not serious, of something light-hearted. It is not exactly laughter, but it is pleasant. Something that is amusing holds our attention and causes us delight. We do not regret it. There is something innocent and lightsome about it.

Or take perhaps a better word, yet one very close in meaning: "recreation." If we break this word down a bit, we see that it contains the word "creation." "Re-creation" means to create again. Aristotle distinguishes between recreation and work. Hannah Arendt, in *The Human Condition,* distinguishes between work and labor; for her, work is what we make, while labor refers to the natural processes of the body, as in the labor pains women have when giving birth. The Latin word for *skole* is *otium*, which means ease or, again, leisure. We seem to need regular "re"-creation in order to return to work, but the end of leisure is to do something for its own sake.

The Latin word for business is *neg-otium*. We use that word in English. We "negotiate" a deal on a car. The idea seems to be that work and business prevent us from leisure, from contemplation and theory, from consideration of the highest things. Slaves and businessmen were not considered part of the polis because the things they did took so much of their time, energy, and effort that they did not have the opportunity to reflect, to consider in any deep fashion.

Even the city itself, in its members, in its political activities, was not constituted in leisure. The city made leisure and its activities—the works of truth, beauty, and the good—possible, but it was not itself this higher purpose. A city needed someone to preserve its soul, someone free from the cares and concerns of political and economic life. Leisure implied that there must be space and time for what was beyond politics, for neither business nor politics seemed to exhaust what we sought.

On the other hand, recreation, and often amusement, referred to the things that someone who works needs to do to go back to work with renewed energy. The end of recreation was indeed more work. The body needs rest and relaxation in order for it to do hard and difficult tasks. Hannah Arendt suggested that labor referred to those necessary and often drudging activities that had to be done so that we could continue living. Garbage had to be collected. Food had to be grown, harvested, and cooked. Houses had constantly to be cleaned or constructed or painted.

"Work," however, can also mean fine arts and crafts. It means making and using. It means not merely keeping alive but making things for the ages. It means taking things from nature and improving on them. Craft and art include both the beautiful and the useful. The things of art and architecture, the monument that Sally wanted to construct, surround us and identify our interior lives in a visible, concrete way.

There is one final notion—besides work, leisure, recreation, business, labor, amusement, and wasted time—that is needed for our discussion. That word is "play," or "sport." We might easily, particularly in light of professional athletics, think of sports as mostly a business, in which case it would be un-leisurely. At first, play or sport seems to be mostly recreation, an escape, a relaxation. But there seems to be something more to it than merely having a relation to work.

A *New Yorker* cartoon once showed a rather startled middle-aged man sitting in his living room watching the evening sportscast on television. The sports announcer reads the following summary of the day's sporting events: "The combined total of major-league batting averages was down three and a half points today. Outs outnumbered hits four to one, on a total volume of fourteen hundred at-bats." Needless to say, we are amused at this treatment of a day of baseball like a day on the stock market. We are aware that the different subject matter makes this a ridiculous comparison: business and sports deal with vastly different subjects, even when there is competition in both.

Aristotle somehow thought that sport or play was more like contemplation than was work or business. He thought that play—say, a championship game—bore some of the characteristics of contemplation. Considering God and considering a game had something in common. Play and contemplation were alike in that both were activities indulged in "for their own sakes," whereas business and work were for something else. Games need not exist, just as the world need not exist, but both do. Aristotle said that sport lacked the seriousness of contemplation. Yet, he did not mean to denigrate the "seriousness" with which we take our games. We are rightly fascinated by them. Even watching a good game can be fascinating. It is its own world and time. It absorbs our attention in something that is not ourselves. Aristotle thought that our relation to God was not unlike that experience.

Once, in the letters of J. R. R. Tolkien, I came across the following passage he wrote in response to the young daughter of one of his publishers who had written to him as part of a school project. She was to write on the question, "What is the purpose in life?" No mean question, of course. Tolkien answered her in this remarkable way:

> The desire to know for the mere sake of knowledge is related to the prayers that some of you address to what you call God. At their highest these seem simply to praise Him for being, as He is, and for making what He has made, as He has made it. Those who believe in a personal God, Creator, do not think the Universe is in itself worshipful, though devoted study of it may be one of the ways to honouring Him. And while as living creatures we are (in part) within it and part of it, our ideas of God and ways of expressing them will be largely derived from contemplating the world about us. (Though there is also revelation both addressed to all men and to particular persons.) So it may be said that the chief purpose of life, for any one of us, is to increase according to our capacity our knowledge of God by all the means we have, and to be moved by it to praise and thanks. To do as we say in the *Gloria in Excelsis: Laudamus te, benedicamus te, adoramus te, glorificamus te, gratias agimus tibi propter magnam gloriam tuam.*[3]

What is striking about this letter to a schoolgirl wanting to know the purpose of life is that Tolkien answered her in terms best understood from sports, that is, that there are things that exist for their own sakes. Cheering and praising have this in common: they are responses to and recognitions of a beauty and glory that is outside us and that we behold.

We should no doubt take our business and our duties seriously. To realize that they do not bear ultimate destiny in themselves, however much we can see the hand of God in them, is not to denigrate them but to accept them for what they are. But when we come to wasted time, to the time we waste with God in prayer or with our friends in laughter and conversation, we begin to approach the essence of that side of faith that reminds us that God is already God.

Tolkien was right. When we understand that God is God, our response is praise, thanks, delight, and joy. That the highest things are for their own sake means that something simply *is*, though we engage in them because we simply want to know about our lives, about why we are. The teaching of Aristotle that play is like contemplation gets at something fundamental: we are—by the important things, by God, by one another, by the games that fascinate us, by beauty and understanding—taken out of ourselves in order to discover what is in some sense also destined to be ours. Joy, Pieper remarked, is the having of what we want, when what we want is itself good and worthy of our fascination, when we receive what we love.

In this sense, Christianity is a religion of "wasted" time. It is a religion of joy because it is a religion of God who is joy. And it tells us that our end is serious joy, because this God is our end. We are to order our lives to participate in the things of this joy—and these are praising and thanking and those activities, as even Plato said, which are manifestations of joy: singing, dancing, even sacrificing. We know that the only time worth having is the time we waste on our friends. And our prayer is the time we "waste" with God, the time we take to comprehend all that is given to us, *all that is.*

INTERLUDE IV

Self-Discipline

EVERYONE HAS HEARD that "all work and no play make Jack a dull boy." Now, I am not exactly sure just who this famous Jack is, but I suspect that in his own way he is each of us when we confront the notion of self-discipline. Clearly, the notion of discipline, especially disciplining one's self, has to do with the systematic process by which we acquire knowledge or virtue or art. Discipline means instruction, especially organized instruction. When we add the notion of "self" to this instruction, we are indicating that we are ourselves objects of our own rule, that we need to instruct ourselves. Ultimately, no one else can do this for us. Our lives are ours to order, to put some sort of principle or purpose into our many and varied thoughts and deeds. Our lives are also ours to leave in disorder or in an order that deviates from what it is we know it ought to be. We should not underestimate the difficulty we confront in ruling ourselves. Christianity even suggests that most of us might well need some help.

This topic is really what Aristotle is getting at in the First Book of the *Ethics* when he tells us to look back reflectively on our deeds and our thoughts to see, if we can, that for which we act, that which we think to be most important and that which governs all we do. No doubt we can mislead ourselves in this reflection. We can think we act for the noblest purposes, whereas in fact, as all our friends know, we act for money or pleasure or vain honors. It is difficult to see ourselves as we are, even though this inner "seeing" is one of the most important things we must do for ourselves. The famous Socratic admonition, "know thyself," means at least that we should strive to have this knowledge of our own implicit ends, as well as to know the kind of being we are by nature—our human nature, which is something we did not give ourselves.

The student who first comes to the university is exhilarated by a kind of newfound freedom. He is still too young really to have acquired a good knowledge of himself or a firm capacity to rule himself. From all I hear, high schools today are not exactly models of balanced preparations for orderly lives. But I suppose, to most high school students, high schools look pretty confined compared to college. No doubt, many young men and women, by the time they reach college, have failed to discipline themselves. They have barely begun to acquire the habits and incentives necessary to figure out, not what they should do in terms of a profession or job, but what life itself is about—itself a lifetime task, to be sure. Many of us, unfortunately, make serious mistakes early in our lives. College is a place in which, if we are wise, these mistakes can be either corrected or, if we are foolish, infinitely magnified.

Now, I am not someone who thinks that we will really learn in college courses what life itself is about. We may get snippets here and there. But universities and colleges are there primarily to be "used." We are not to attend them blindly, even though we can and must make ourselves teachable. For a good number of the very important books and ideas that a student will need to know if he is to know the truth, and if he is to confront what is good, are never mentioned in any university curriculum or course. This situation implies that we need to know something about life even before we learn more specifically about parts of it in an academic setting. If we are lucky, we begin to suspect that some of these things we need to know, the highest things, can be learned from our parents or our church or our friends or our own curiosity. Many a man has saved his soul because of some book he chanced to read in some obscure library or used bookstore. Many a girl has understood what her life is about because she happened, one random summer afternoon, to talk seriously to her grandmother or to her aunt.

Self-discipline—the ability to rule over all our given passions, fears, dreams, and thoughts—can be, if simply taken for itself, a dangerous thing. We can be Stoics who conceive self-discipline somehow as its own end, whereas it is really the prerequisite for seeing and loving what is not ourselves. Nonetheless, our ability to accomplish anything at all begins with the realization that we must take control of ourselves. We must begin to note in ourselves those things that cause us troubles. These difficulties can even be other students, perhaps even teachers, who interfere with our studies or our responsibilities, including our responsibilities to God. They can be things like drink or drugs or our own laziness.

The object of self-discipline, then, in the best sense, is not the self. That may sound strange. The classical writers used to relate self-discipline to liberty. The person who was most free was the one who had the most control over himself. The person who was most unfree was the one who was ruled by pleasures, money, or power. Self-discipline does not, however, solve the question of what is knowledge or truth or good. In this sense, it is instrumental, something good for the sake of something else. John Paul II put it well in *Crossing the Threshold of Hope*: "the fundamental dimension of man's existence...is always a co-existence."[1] We are supposed to rule ourselves. But once we have managed to approach this no doubt difficult task, what remains is the rest of our lives. We can then begin to focus on the things of the highest importance and dignity, something we would be unable to do if we did not succeed in imposing some discipline on ourselves. Paul Johnson, in *Intellectuals*, put forth the considerably unpopular thesis that there is an intimate connection between our moral lives and our intellectual lives.[2] Sometimes I think the history of our times can be described as an argument about whether or not this connection is true; Classical and Christian thought, of course, hold that it is. Self-discipline is the beginning of wisdom, but not its end. When we have accomplished the initial task of self-discipline, we will, if we are sane, hardly recall it, for it will have freed us to see so much else.

CHAPTER 8

※

On the Teaching of Political Philosophy

But these truths are too important to be new....

— SAMUEL JOHNSON, *Rasselas*

STUDENTS WONDER what their professors actually hold, I think. Deeds are often as revealing as words, of course, and together they indicate what we are. I am conscious of the fact that as a young professor, I was still trying to figure out what indeed it was that I held. Part of the advantage—and the danger—of being a teacher is that you are actually given time to pursue the truth. It is by no means easy to know what one's own students think, even when you grade their papers and read their essays. They themselves often do not know either. The very meaning of being a student is to be on the road to knowing but not yet to have arrived. We are intended to become mature, to cease being students, to arrive at contemplation, an "activity" that does not cease.

Teaching is not an exact science, something for which we all can be thankful. Rather, teaching is an overflow of the truth of existing things now affirmed in our souls. This truth is presented to souls no doubt equally as intelligent as teachers and equally as desirous to know, if not more so. St. Thomas remarked that the nobility of teaching was *contemplata tradere*, that is, to pass on to others the things we have first contemplated in our own souls. This "passing on" demands that we systematically, earnestly, and wisely do seek to know, to ponder the truth of things. This contemplation is the one thing that we owe to ourselves and our students. The truth we know, moreover, is not exclusively "ours." When students learn the same truth we have taken so long to learn, we are not less, though they are more. "Humility is truth," as the spiritual writers used to say to this point. The spiritual things that spiritual beings know are free.

I want to write something here that is within the context of political philosophy, yet related to the theme of the "unseriousness of human affairs" with which this book is primarily concerned. The very nature of political philosophy seems to encourage it. That is, political philosophy gives rise to certain ultimate questions that lead beyond political philosophy, including friendship, death, evil, reward, punishment, sacrifice, the good, the truth, justice, courage, love, and generosity.[1] Revelation responds to these same questions in a startling but uncanny way. From a rational point of view, it seems to be a coincidence that these things, philosophy and revelation, should relate to each other. I do not intend to deny the multiple conflicting voices that claim to speak for the same revelation, nor the fact that there are radically different religions. In fact, political philosophy, because of the questions it provokes, requires us to ask which understanding of religion and revelation provides the best answer to those questions. This requirement, if you will, is the service philosophy provides for revelation.

But I recognize also that it is a doctrinal position of the Christian faith, at least, that philosophy, however legitimate and persuasive, will not see the necessity of this connection between itself and revelation, though it can feel its attraction and wonder about it. Indeed, it is actually "heretical" to hold that reason can see, and fully account for, all the essential truths of revelation, particularly those which relate to the inner life of

God and to the Incarnation of God within history. Were reason able to arrive at the knowledge of the highest things by its own powers alone, we would already be gods. We would not need anything more than our own intelligences to know *all that is*; however, this seems obviously not to be the case. Likewise, it is "heretical" to maintain that there are "two truths," one from reason and one from revelation, which can contradict each other yet both be "true." Revelation and reason belong to the same universe. We cannot have it otherwise.

It is not impossible to philosophize properly while at the same time accepting the fact that revelation, when looked at for what it actually maintains, is addressed to real human beings through its answers to problems that legitimately arise in political philosophy. Political philosophy has a certain natural priority to both philosophy and revelation because a polity may decide to interfere with our pursuit of these questions and because certain enigmas appear in every society. Political philosophy must persuade the politician to allow us to think, but there are issues about which we must think, issues that the polity neither creates nor removes.

Callicles, the intelligent and smooth politician, is present in every society, as Plato intimated in his *Gorgias*. He indulgently pats the philosopher on the head in the name of empty but powerful local culture over which the politician rules. Unlike Aristotle, Callicles ominously tells the philosopher not to worry too much about unsettling philosophical dilemmas. They are not worth the trouble. Callicles will take care of all the really important things. The political philosopher, if he listens, is charmed, flattered, or coerced out of his heritage. In the view of Callicles, Socrates, over in the corner with the beardless youth, is merely talking nonsense. Thus, with Callicles in control, the highest things go unattended. They will not touch the politician's own soul, and therefore the polity will be most dangerous. It is to correct this inattention, I think, that the academy exists. But when the academy, as it often does, betrays its own vocation, what must take its place is the particular teacher: Socrates and, as St. Thomas thought, revelation itself (ST, I-II, 91, 4).

After many years of teaching and writing, I realize that my students are not only those whom I know and remember with some delight and affection from class, but also those who may have read something I wrote. Sometimes, in fact, they are the same people, as I have often assigned my own texts to my hapless, long-suffering students. I found that when I was a student there was something salutary about reading what my teacher had written, or in listening to what any writer had to say if I happened to have the opportunity.

When one writes, however, he writes for "the world." In a classroom, student and teacher are eye-to-eye, so to speak. But when we write, we never know if anyone is out there. A friend of mine told me once that it was quite possible that before my career ended, "you will teach more students in class than you will ever find readers for what you write, especially academic stuff." Nevertheless, I once received a letter from a man I had never heard of—a working man in Brisbane, Australia—who thanked me for some obscure book I had written on social philosophy, which he had found in the back of his local church. In the highest of things, an audience of one is sufficient—which, after all, is what Aristotle meant when he said that we could have only a few friendships of the best kind.

Teaching has a certain advantage over writing because both teacher and pupil are before each other. Physical presence inevitably reveals things that the written word never could. Personalities, preparations, responses are there to be encountered. Writing, however, is more permanent in that it is there to read again, to be pondered more slowly. Writing may be more revealing in other ways. Most of the great writers are in their graves, but we can still meet them, as I have pointed out several times, in their books. The greatest teachers, Socrates and Christ, never wrote a word. But we encounter their stories and words because someone *did* write about them. And through those words, we must not forget, we are intended to reach nothing less than reality.

So do professors actually believe the things they write about or teach in class? As Leo Strauss remarked, there is a certain circumspection that one must employ before he decides to state what he thinks is true.[2] Ideologically, the modern university—not to mention the modern state and media—is astonishingly conformist. Tocqueville was on to something when he worried that democracy might be the most conformist of all regimes. One speaks of the highest things in university and polity at some peril. Writing is often freer because one can publish in different countries, in different climates of opinion, and for different audiences, even though writing is more permanent.

There is an intimate relationship between teaching and writing. Teaching often stimulates writing, though it need not. Teaching gives a professor the opportunity to present again and again over the years the matter that he is concerned about. Students may be seeing something for the first time, whereas the professor is seeing it for the fiftieth. It is one of the joys of political philosophy, however, that the fiftieth reading can be as exciting as the first, and is often more so. Indeed, as often happens, the first reading may well be drudgery. How frequently do I find a student who will come up after class to tell me that he does not "like" Aristotle, this after his having hurriedly read but once in his whole short life only the first seven books of the *Ethics!* I never fail to look most pained when I hear this complaint, because in fact I am most pained. But I recall reading Plato for the first time, and the second, and the third, when he seemed as unintelligible to me as Aristotle to my student. About the fiftieth time, he began to make some sense. Students going through Plato for the first time at my behest provide me the opportunity to go through Plato for the fifty-first time. It is a fair deal, I am happy to think.

Yet, it is one thing to teach the truth and another to live it. Students want to know about the unity of life. We all know it is possible for professors—perhaps especially for professors (and clerics)—to teach one thing and act in a contrary manner. This sort of conduct does not necessarily mean that what they teach is wrong. "On the chair of Moses have sat the Scribes and the Pharisees," Christ warned, "do what they teach, not as they live."

We are all in some sense sinners. At times, we knowingly act contrary to what is right and knowingly fail to tell or write the truth. Indeed, I argue that one of the recurring issues we must confront in life, an issue with political overtones, is evil: what is it? How is it that we do it ourselves? We remain human when we perform any evil act, and some will maintain that this fallibility or sinfulness is the first and surest sign of humanity.[3] I would be the first to acknowledge that we are all imperfect, all in some sense capable of acting unjustly or greedily or violently, even when we think it wrong to do so. The Fall, whatever we make of it, is more a fact than a theory.

The young, because they lack experience, are less capable of understanding this darker side of human nature than the old professors who have seen it all, even in themselves. Aristotle said as much in the *Ethics*, when he remarked that the young are not yet suitable students of ethical and political matters. This lack of experience need not mean that young potential philosophers ought not to attend to what the philosophers say about what they will, in due time, most likely do or think. Indeed, helping the young see this is one of the genuine services teachers can perform; they should forewarn students so that when the time comes for them to fail as most others have failed, they will not be too discouraged.

But neither professors nor students should be content in the knowledge that they are, in evil, just like everyone else. It is not accidental that topics of forgiveness, salvation, and redemption arise naturally from our own experience of what we in fact do. But such questions may not arise at once. We are given a "complete life," as Aristotle puts it, for a reason. For most of us, it takes a long time to be ready to cope with what we in fact do—and with what others do to us.

But in spite of all that might be said about death, evil, pain, and even Hell, pleasure, happiness, and joy are much more intellectually difficult and profound things to account for—and even defend—than any of these more dire topics. When we realize this, we really will have begun to come to grips with the realities about which political philosophy causes us to wonder. It is no accident that these topics are found in Plato and Aristotle, in the Gospels, in St. Augustine and St. Thomas, even in modernity.

The essential purpose of political philosophy is serious, even though there may be a higher seriousness, as I have been suggesting. Students arrive in inchoate intellectual shape before a professor. They are ritually embarrassed if someone affirms that something can be true or right, that something is evil, that most of the current enthusiasms for which students and politicians stake their lives are ideological in nature. Students with such relativist persuasions are even less prepared to hear that some polities, even their own, are better or worse than others, that it does make a difference what we think and do, that what we do does proceed from what we think, that the truth alone will make us free, that some things just won't work whatever we do.

These same students are quite surprised, even sometimes pleased, to learn that the purpose of thinking is not just thinking but thinking the truth. They are relieved to be told, finally, that the purpose of truth is that we should live according to it, that we will not be happy unless we "know ourselves." Students are happy to realize that we have not and cannot "create" or "make" what constitutes our blessedness, that it is simply up to us whether we choose to achieve it.

But I have no intention of "imposing" my views by stating what they are. To the uninterested student, I talk about the weather, itself a worthy topic. (Chesterton said that there are no *uninteresting* subjects, only *uninterested* people. This remark, while even applicable to topics like turtles or rocks, is even truer of the highest things.) For one thing, I do not think that classical arguments and conclusions, if they are true—or even if they are false, for that matter—are simply "my" views. I am not a follower of modernity; that is, if I know a truth, it is not because I believe I made it to be true, but because I discovered it in something I did not make, in a reality which was there before me. If any of my views are true, they are potentially everyone's views, but only if we all proceed through the process by which they can be seen to be true. It is possible to waste a lot of time coming to knowledge of the highest things, even though "wasted time" is sometimes our most valuable time, as I intimated in an earlier chapter.

We can easily get distracted by how we live, as the young Augustine explains in a text, his *Confessions,* that still speaks familiarly to the soul of every young student. Or we might never be confronted with a guide who tells us about Plato or Aristotle or Aquinas because our polity or university does not allow or encourage them. The claim is that what they have to say does not transcend their status as Greeks, or worse, male theologians. They need not be taken seriously. No disease of the modern soul is more fatal than this, I think.

We should intend in our souls to pursue truth. But not a truth that stands outside of the argument in which it was achieved. Even revelation is intended to make us think correctly. We want to be open enough to allow for considerations that might arrive from outside of philosophy but are nonetheless related to its purposes. The student should not be afraid to consider the classical texts that today are often, until read, the most unpopular ones. It is my experience that the classic books and the ideas that flow out of them are capable of being assimilated in the soul of anyone who thinks his way through them. I do not just mean undertaking a perfunctory reading of a "great author" or "great book." Rather, I mean allowing the author to point out in us, in our own lives if he can, what it is he is talking about. Ultimately, if we do not see it there, we read in vain. When Socrates on his last day sat with his young friends, he chided them for weeping at his fate when he had tried so hard to teach them what it was proper to weep about. When reading Socrates through the eyes of the young Plato, it is not sufficient to "understand" from the outside what he said. We should try to see that Socrates speaks to the trouble in our own souls. We should realize that Socrates is still teaching us.

I claim the liberty to teach about questions that arise in political philosophy by virtue of what it is in itself. For example, in Aristotle, God seems to be lacking something noble that belongs to human beings: friendship. Friendship in Aristotle's view was what principally held cities together, and it was the context in which the highest things we know exist. And therefore I must treat this wonderful topic in political philosophy.[4] Clearly, the Aristotelian First Mover, even though he moves by love and desire, seems to lack care for human beings and for the world. If this is true, there is a deep problem here, both in political philosophy and in being itself, a problem we cannot avoid if we seek to know *all that is.*

If we accumulate all of the intricate problems that do arise in an Aristotle and other philosophers, we might think that the world was ill made. This view seems reasonable enough and many a philosopher has held it. But if there is an "otherness" in God, as revelation maintains, it might not be so easy to exclude friendship from Him. The highest things that even human beings know might not be lacking in God, in other words. This unified otherness in the divinity really would make it less difficult to see why friendship is so important to us, why we are said to be made in God's "image." Moreover, this otherness in God might indicate that what was not God was in fact not necessary to God's completion, whereas many philosophers postulated this lack to be the reason for the existence of something other than God. I remark on these things not to persuade anyone of the curious coincidence of ideas found here but to insist that such considerations must at least be considered in political philosophy. After all, the questions that ultimately provoke their consideration initially arose in this discipline.

Socrates remarked in the *Republic* that he loved Homer and was charmed by him, but that he did not find many of his stories true. He found some of them dangerous, in fact. Plato knew that to overcome the charm of Homer merely through dry philosophy was an impossible task, a truth attested to by many a student. The only way Plato knew by which he might accomplish the task of overcoming the lethargy that philosophy usually generates would be to write a philosophic tale that was itself more charming than Homer.[5] But to know whether the *Republic*, the tale that

Plato wrote, accomplishes this task, we must first be charmed by Homer himself. Indeed, we must wonder, with Chesterton, why there is anything at all, and why we love to know about it.[6]

I have suggested over the years certain texts to be read carefully in order to charm the student or the random reader into realizing that the questions about the highest things are found in the structure of his very being. These books and readings have also charmed me.[7] Furthermore, I am, if not charmed, at least provoked by certain purely abstract questions: what would happen if there were a truth? What is evil? Why are we punished? How is it that something conforms to what we want? How do I rule myself? Are we alone in the universe? Who is my friend? What is the best regime? Where do I find it? Why does man learn by suffering? How can I repair the evils I have done? Does suffering have a purpose? Are we made for joy?

But it is not enough to be charmed or provoked, however necessary and legitimate these might be. After we have marveled at the tales in the *Republic* and been moved by the friendship that an Aristotle or a Cicero found to be at the root of our being, after we know that we must die, if not by hemlock or the Cross, at least in bed, we still must formulate the serious questions. We exist as beings who are questioned by life and death itself, though we are so distracted and so busy that we do not often have time to confront the highest things. Sometimes, if we are fortunate, our polity in its education—or, as Solzhenitsyn seemed to suggest, even in its imprisonments—will allow a few moments for such a confrontation.

Many alternative candidates will clamor for our attention, however, as Aristotle told us in the First Book of the *Ethics.* Plato was also correct when he admonished us that we cannot afford to make a mistake about the highest things because we have only one lifetime in which to get it right. We will need a teacher. Leo Strauss said, in a passage I cited earlier, that we are lucky if two or three of the greatest minds that have ever lived are alive when we are. He was sober enough to add that the teachers who are considered the greatest do not always agree with each other.[8] And we should be patient if we discover along the way that the greatest of teachers drank hemlock or was executed by a Roman governor in an obscure province because he claimed to be God.

The last question that political philosophy asks, I suppose, is whether it all fits together, the contemplative happiness and the political happiness of which Aristotle spoke in the last book of the *Ethics*. This question is surely the one that most bothers the young potential philosopher when he sets out on his path. It still bothers the professor when he nears the end. Adeimantus and Glaucon, in the Second Book of the *Republic*, earnestly called Socrates aside and wanted to have him explain privately to them the case for justice. They did this because, in spite of all evidence from their experience and schooling to the contrary, they still hoped that all things did fit together. For this information they only knew one place to go, namely, to the philosopher, to Socrates. Socrates was touched by their persistent efforts to discover what was true. And besides Socrates, there might still be one more place to go. We should at least test it.

If I am asked, "Does it all fit together?" I am ready to say that it does, provided we are willing to pursue the question. The trouble with most arguments, as Chesterton remarks, is that they are too short. They end before they have time to work their own logic out. I think it is possible to conduct a search through the great texts for an understanding of the highest things. I know that the student has to begin, and the best place for him to begin is with the texts in which the highest things are discussed. I know that he may not at first know they *are* the highest things, but he will if he continues, and yes, if he loves *what is*.

I also recall Plato's charm. I recall Adeimantus and Glaucon, who wanted Socrates to tell them the truth because if he didn't, they despaired of finding anyone else who would. I recall the two Apostles who, when they had met Christ, came to see where he lived, dropping their fishing nets to become fishers of men. And I know that if we read good things, we have a chance. But I also know about evil, about our souls, and about the Fall. We must be realists without being relativists.

In the pursuit of political philosophy, the serious student, like the aging professor, will find that this discipline is surely one way to reach the truth of things if he is willing to allow the subject matter to carry him to its own ending. Not without reason did Aristotle note that the first question in political philosophy is, "What is happiness?" When, in Book Six of the *Republic*, Socrates stopped speaking of justice and began to speak of "the good," he set political philosophy in pursuit of the highest things. The pursuit continues in the hearts of all who read such texts, especially those, like the young Augustine, who are both charmed and perplexed by the questions that arise. As young philosophers grow older, they may suspect, if they are fortunate, that the proper answers are more joyful and more realistic than even the learned texts have intimated.[9]

Political philosophy at its best, I think, still passes from the *Republic* to the *City of God*. This position—at least for those who wonder about what I might hold—is the heart of the matter. The journey to the truth passes through the cell where Socrates spent his last days and the Cross on which Christ hung. It also passes through the experience of modernity. That is, political philosophy is aware, in its highest reaches, of the states that kill philosophers, teachers, and saints. The charm of political philosophy is a sober charm. But we would be foolish to miss it.

"If [a professor] does not 'write' this text [what he has learned] down in one way or another," Frederick Wilhelmsen wrote, " he is not a professor because he has nothing personal to say about his subject."[10] So what I have to say is written down. I hope it is not another essay composed of the "brilliant errors" of which Strauss wrote, the errors that too often compose the content of academic political philosophy.[11]

Let my last words be those of Samuel Johnson. But this time, in their abiding wisdom, let them be mediated in the light of the *Republic*, the *Ethics*, the trials of Socrates and Christ, the *City of God*, and, yes, even *The Prince* of Machiavelli and the *Leviathan* of Hobbes: "The inseparable imperfections annexed to all human governments consisted in not being able to create a sufficient fund of virtue and principle to carry the laws into due and effectual execution. Wisdom might plan, but virtue alone could execute."[12] Brilliant errors, indeed.

I am, I confess, charmed by such things. This is what I must confess to my students and to my readers, potential philosophers all, whose purpose is, and can be nothing less than, the truth of things. The path by way of political philosophy is but one way to the highest things. But it is a real way for those of us who are doomed indeed to die but also admonished to wonder about friendship with God and with one another, even by him whom St. Thomas called "the Philosopher," even by the discourse at the last Supper. If we do not yet know these things, they are there to be known. "These truths are too important to be new," as Johnson remarked. And that too is what I hold.

CHAPTER 9

On the Pleasure of Walking About Derby

I

No ONE WILL EVER KNOW whether there are answers to the highest questions unless he has first accurately formulated the very questions to which such answers might be addressed. Faith does depend on reason in this sense, that reason need not exclude *a priori* those answers of revelation that curiously seem to be aware of the abiding questions, when accurately formulated.

A cartoon in the *New Yorker* puts us in a wealthy businessman's club on Wall Street.[1] Two gleefully sardonic bankers are talking to each other over their morning paper. Both are bald, portly, and attired in very conservative suits. With a wicked gleam in his eyes, the first man, who obviously practices what he preaches, turns to the second man, who listens with knowing approval. "Sure, life isn't fair," he says, "but that's all right." Clearly, the cartoon implies that it was the unfairness of life that enabled these two successful bankers to garner and enjoy all those good things about them.

But is life fair? Is it all right if it isn't? And if it isn't, whose fault is it? Ours? God's? Can we find some scapegoat for our ills—society, say, or the environment, or the rich, or even fate? What can we hope for? Will the world ever become perfect? When? Where? Would we in our fallibility recognize it if it did become perfect? Is the world related to us? Are we the world "writ" small, as Plato said? Are fairness and unfairness due to our own choices? Are all of us but "reeds shaken in the wind?"—to recall Christ's ironic words about John the Baptist?

In 1980, Eric Voegelin engaged in a series of conversations with students and faculty at the Thomas More Institute in Montreal. I often find myself repeating these conversations. During the course of these wonderful exchanges, Voegelin was asked the anxious question we all have asked at one time or another, "But what are we to *do* about the problems of the world?" Voegelin's response has always seemed to me to indicate a basic insight into the intellectual life. It is not an affirmation of individualism, nor of collectivism, nor is it a sort of skepticism that satisfies itself that in knowing that we know nothing—contrary to Socrates—we in fact *can* know nothing.

Voegelin's advice to potential philosophers was this: "Civilizations as such are never static because every man is a new element of revolution in the world. Just stop being static and do something.... Nobody is obliged to participate in the crisis of his time. He can do something else."[2] The first thing we can do, then, is refuse to cooperate with the forces that have brought upon us a crisis of culture.

Such a response is grounded in the memory of events handed down in our tradition. In the *Apology* of Socrates, we read about the case of Leon of Salamis. This notorious case was the only time Socrates, the private citizen and philosopher, was asked to act as a public official. Leon, it seems, was one of ten Athenian generals who, in 406 B.C., had failed to gather up the bodies of the fallen after the Battle of Arginusaie. The proud Athenians were angry and wanted to try these men for treason en masse, contrary to Athenian law. In order to carry out their designs, they appointed five armed men, including Socrates, to go over to Salamis and pick up Leon. When it came time to depart, four citizens went to fetch

Leon, but Socrates, as he tells us, "went home." He did not participate in the crisis of his time.

In Book II of the *Republic*, we encounter a not dissimilar scene involving Adeimantus and Glaucon, Plato's brothers, who want to hear virtue praised for its own sake. Socrates listens to these two earnest and impressive young men. Whether they will be attracted by the highest things, what they will do with their freedom and life, neither yet knows. Both know, however, that the best of men can become the worst. Indeed, in a majority of cases it seems likely that this dire result will occur. Socrates is astonished to hear them vividly expound the case for injustice in such eloquent and philosophical terms. But he is even more startled to learn that they are not persuaded by their own arguments. They are attracted by the good even when they cannot defend or explain it.

Then there is the account in the New Testament of the rich young man (Luke 18:18-27). He is not unlike Adeimantus and Glaucon. He questions the philosopher. He wants to know about the highest things. He has kept the Commandments from his youth. He asks Christ what he must do to be perfect. In a response not unrelated to the scene described in the Fifth Book of the *Republic*, in which all temptations are removed from the guardians, Christ tells the wealthy young man that he must go and sell what he has, give it to the poor, and follow the Lord.[3] "But when he heard these answers," St. Luke tells us, "he went away sad." It seems incredible to believe that we can have all things, be virtuous, desire the good, and still be asked to do more. We go away sadly; we begin to think that life is not fair.

At Agincourt, Henry offered to pay passage home for those of his soldiers who wished to return to England before the battle. Just as those who returned to England could not in their old age recount what happened on that St. Crispin's Day, the rich young man could not reflect, later in life, on the exciting journeys he would have taken had he stayed with the Lord. And yet, if the cause had been ignoble, they would have been right not to participate. In *Nobody's Perfect, Charlie Brown*, a book with obviously Platonic overtones, Charlie is reading from a scientific report in the morning newspaper. Lucy is looking away, rather bored. "It says here," Charlie begins, "that the force of gravitation is 13% less today than it was 4 billion years ago...." Lucy, on hearing this otherwise useless bit of information, suddenly turns on Charlie to snap, "Whose fault is that?" "Whose fault is it?" Charlie, somewhat taken aback, protests, "It's nobody's fault." His moral placidity before fate sends Lucy into a rage. While Charlie forlornly listens, looking down at the paper, she yells, "What do you mean nobody's fault! It HAS to be somebody's fault! Somebody's got to take the blame!" Finally, she opens her mouth wide, throws up her arms, and screams at Charlie, turning him upside down, "FIND A SCAPEGOAT!" For Lucy, the world isn't fair. It's ill-made. And somebody must pay.

Two of the most significant words in the English language are nearly homophonic—to "wonder" and to "wander." The first word, wonder, suggests something about our minds, about the extraordinary fact that we want to know and that we are satisfied only when we do know. To know is its own sort of pleasure, as Aristotle told us. Nowhere is this fact about ourselves stated more clearly than in the conversation in Book III of the *Republic*. To Glaucon, the young and potential philosopher who is not sure whether he will choose the good, Socrates says, "Isn't being deceived about the truth bad, and to have the truth good? Or isn't it your opinion that to affirm the things *that are*, is to have the truth?" (413a) To these profound questions, Glaucon admits, "What you say is correct." We do not wonder simply to wonder, but to know the truth and to affirm it.

"To wander," on the other hand, has special overtones. It touches on aim and aimlessness. Another *New Yorker* cartoon takes us to a psychiatrist's office.[4] On the couch, flat on his back, hands folded, legs crossed, nervously twitching, lies a very large chicken. The psychiatrist, notebook in hand, turns to the chicken to ask, "Why do *you* cross the road?" Why do any of us go where we go? Do boundaries make a difference? "Why are we homesick even at home?" Chesterton asks. We wander because we have here no lasting city.

Several years ago, a friend sent me from England an early French edition of Madame de Sévigné's letters. Madame de Sévigné's letter from Bourbilly on October 16, 1673, to her daughter reads:

> Enfin, ma chère fille, j'arrive présentement dans le vieux château de mes pères. J'ai trouvé mes belle prairies, ma petite rivière et mon beau moulin, à la même place où je les avois laissés. Il y a eu ici de plus honnêtes gens que moi; et cependant, au sortir de Grignan, je m'y meurs de tristesse [Finally, my dear daughter, I am presently arriving in the old chateau of my fathers. I have found my lovely fields, my small stream, and my lovely mill, at the same place where I left them. Here there were perhaps more upright people than I, but nevertheless, on going out from Grignan, I died of sadness].[5]

This letter serves to remind us not merely of wandering and returning but of the effect that place, especially a happy place that we have loved, can have on our souls. If we are sad, it is sometimes not because life is not fair but because life is so dear, full of the lovely fields, streams, and beautiful mills of nostalgic remembrance.

The famous Western novelist Louis L'Amour began in 1930 to make long lists of the books he read. In that year, the first three books were by George Santayana, followed by Joseph Conrad's *Selected Stories* and Friedrich Schleiermacher's *Soliloquies.* I have a certain affinity with such an enterprise, I must confess. Perhaps the only thing that will save us from the many ideologies found in academia and public life will be books—good books—that we find lying about unnoticed because, as was the situation in the Athenian democracy, virtually no one can now distinguish a good book from a silly one.

But as ways to truth, I would not exclude prayer, nor would I neglect the possibility that in our wanderings about this world we might just meet good men and women, people who can tell us more than any mere philosopher or academic. We are called, in fact, by St. Peter in his Epistle, "wayfarers and pilgrims"; and at the end of the Synoptic Gospels, we are said to have a mission, to be sent along a way to all the nations, to the ends of the world. That there is indeed something to be said to all men, in all times, and in all cultures, is the ground of the claim of universal civilization itself.

Thus, as Aristotle also hinted, it might just be possible to find the truth through encounters with those particular people who live good lives, like the parents of Madame de Sévigné in Grignan. To the same point, L'Amour wrote, "I know that no university exists that can provide an education; what a university can provide is an outline, to give the learner a direction and a guidance. The rest one has to do for oneself."[6] If we think that a university will automatically "educate" us, we will seek scapegoats when we find that we are not educated—if indeed we ever find this out, for to know we know nothing, we need the capacity to know, as Socrates consistently maintained.

II

On Friday, September 19, 1777, Dr. Johnson and James Boswell set out in the Rev. Dr. John Taylor's post-chaise for Derby, North of Birmingham. On the way, they stopped by Keddlestone, the seat of Lord Scarsdale. A fine house was found there. "I was struck with the magnificence of the buildings; and the extensive park, with the finest verdure, covered with deer, and cattle, and sheep, delighted me," Boswell wrote. He found there wonderful old oaks and a fine gravel road and ponds and a lovely Gothic church. Thinking of this magnificence—and not unmindful of the Rich Young Man, which he himself was—Boswell confesses that this "grand group of objects agitated and distended my mind in a most agreeable manner. 'One should think (said I), that the proprietor of all this must be happy.'"

Samuel Johnson was listening intently to this account. With great profundity, he replied to Boswell, "Nay, Sir, all this [vast property] excludes but one evil—poverty."[7] Johnson knew that the deepest human unhappiness can and does exist in the most well-appointed and prosperous seats of culture, something we learned from Plato in Athens, Christ in Jerusalem, and St. Paul in Rome, yet a truth that modernity seems loathe to admit.

The party proceeded on towards Derby. The post-chaise seems to have been a speedy one. Johnson, not unlike the future drivers of Porsches on German autobahns and Corvettes on Los Angeles freeways, liked to drive very fast. Boswell records him as even admitting that "If I had no duties, and no reference to futurity, I would spend my life in driving briskly in a post-chaise with a pretty woman; but she should be one who could understand us, and would add something to the conversation."[8] When the post-chaise finally arrived in Derby, Boswell had a chance to see the local sights. "I felt a pleasure in walking about Derby such as I always have in walking about any town to which I am not accustomed," Boswell reflected. "There is an immediate sensation of novelty; and one speculates on the way in which life is passed in it, which, although there is a sameness every where upon the whole, is yet minutely diversified. The minute diversities in every thing are wonderful."[9] The general constancy of human nature across time and space is recorded here. But the particularities of human existence are, indeed, "wonderful," as Boswell remarked. The same sentiment exists in Dante, St. Paul, Aristotle, Plato, and perhaps originally in Herodotus.

III

One of the joys of teaching is that students, over the years, have given me books I might not otherwise have seen or read. They seem to know books or essays their somewhat odd professor will especially like—how I am never quite sure, but they are usually right. Years ago, a graduate student saw a copy of Boswell's *Life of Johnson* in a used bookstore in Miami. He bought it for me for a couple of dollars because I had read something of Johnson in class. I still read a little of it almost every day. Its charm has not lessened. Life is too short to comprehend it all, I think.

A young lady who is now in the diplomatic corps once sent me a copy of T. H. White's *The Once and Future King*, a book I did not know. Early in the book, under the instructions of Merlyn the magician, Kay, the future king, and the Wart, his young friend, are being taught to hunt rabbits. Both Kay and Wart have six arrows, and one Thursday afternoon Kay manages to hit a rabbit. Kay and Wart clean it with a hunting knife. As they prepared to go home, the boys had one further exercise: "Every Thursday afternoon, after the last serious arrow had been shot, they were allowed to fit one more hock into their strings and to shoot the arrow straight up into the air. It was partly a gesture of farewell, partly of triumph, and it was beautiful. They did it now to salute their first prey."[10] This is the sign of the human being, that he can not only shoot the rabbit for training and for food, but also can shoot an arrow into the air and see that it is beautiful. Wandering about the fields leads to wondering about how beautiful things can be. At the end of need and necessity lie freedom and loveliness.

Another student gave me a book that, while not exactly a challenge to *The Closing of the American Mind*, does contain a certain educational wisdom: Robert Fulghum's *All I Really Need to Know I Learned in Kindergarten*. Yet I am quite sure that the proposition of the title is not true, if only because I never went to kindergarten. Many of the best things I know I seem to have learned only lately.

Perhaps we should recall Aristotle's wonder here, that the things that are best to know are not necessarily those we "need" to know but those we find most enchanting because we do not need them. The final question I always ask of myself and of my students is simply, "What do you do when all else is done?" Unless we can broach an answer to such a question, our lives will necessarily be incomplete and not a little sad. And the answer, I think, has something to do with the arrow shot into the air.

Fulghum recounts this story:

There was a famous French criminologist named Emile Locard, and fifty years ago he came up with something called Locard's Exchange

Principle. It says something to the effect that any person passing through a room will unknowingly deposit something there and take something away. Modern technology proves it. Fulghum's Exchange Principle extends it: Every person passing through this life will unknowingly leave something and take something away. Most of this "something" cannot be seen or heard or numbered. It does not show up in a census. But nothing counts without it.[11]

This reflection reminds me of a passage from E. F. Schumacher's *A Guide for the Perplexed*, a book I read frequently with my classes. Schumacher remarks that when we look at other human beings as a class or group, without in the least denying our corporeality, all the really important things about them are invisible to us. We have to cultivate our inner lives to be able to understand what is going on within someone else.[12]

A couple of years ago, a tall young man came by my office. He wore a rather scraggly beard, and somehow I felt I knew him, though I could not place him. He told me that he had been "wandering over Europe." He had been to France and Germany and I do not know where all during the previous year. And he had spent about three months on Mt. Athos, that extraordinary complex of monasteries in the Orthodox tradition built on the most famous and most spiritually important mountain in Eastern Christianity.

I asked this former student why he had wandered so about the world. "It was that book you assigned," he told me. "What book?" I asked. "The Schumacher book—you see, I am Greek. It was the first time I ever read anything that made me wonder what this Greek tradition meant and how it was deeply meaningful and valid." Schumacher's profound unease with his own education at Oxford, its failure to address the things that were really important, still resonated, apparently.

The final book I was given about which I wish to comment was given to me by a perceptive young graduate student from Mexico City: Denis de Rougemont's *Love in the Western World*.[13] This book, the student told me, "saved my life from the pervasive Hegelianism which is everywhere present at the University of Mexico." Rougemont takes up the gnostic problem in Western culture—the notion of self-salvation and the denigration of matter—an issue about which Eric Voegelin has made us aware. He reminds us that the struggle against the Manicheans in our midst is by no means over.

Rougemont's thesis is that it is the Incarnation that saves the world, marriage, and passion. But Gnosticism, which denies the Incarnation, pervades much modern thought and literature. The primacy of death over life that Rougemont studied confirms my long-held suspicion that the purpose of philosophy and the university in general is to prepare us to ask the right questions. We are question-making beings, and this is as it should be. Yet, if we are question-making beings, even more are we answer-receiving beings. We cannot have one without the other without, ultimately, contradicting ourselves.

We live in an ideological time that proudly assures us that no answers can be given, that there is only power and exploitation and contingency. No proposition is more questionable or less questioned than this. But it is not true that there are no answers. What *is* true is that there are many answers we are not prepared to recognize because we have not formulated the proper questions. What *is* true, and consequently ominous, is that we can choose not to question because we do not want to hear the answer. We do not want to change our lives. And as Plato said, a lie in the soul is the worst of evils.

The answers to the most profound questions are suggested by those faces and localities that we have come to know. The loss of these very things, when they are no longer incarnate among us, will cause that sadness of heart that Madame de Sévigné recalled. Both the faces we know and the old streets that are new to us, along with the beauty of the unserious arrow shot straight up into the air on a Thursday afternoon, form the beginning of the answers to the deepest questions, which are properly addressed to the love of *what is*—in the Western world or any other.

INTERLUDE V

The End of All Things

"Before" anything begins, God *is*. That is, God stands outside of nothingness. God is all complete, existing with an inner Trinitarian life that needs no world, no man, no angel. If anything but God exists, it is not because something is deficient or lonely in God. What is not God cannot explain itself to itself without God. *God's purpose in creation is to associate other knowing beings—angels and men—with His inner life.* This purpose never changes. No "natural" angelic or human condition ever in fact existed, even though it might have. That is, both angels and men were, from the beginning, intended to be more than their nature allowed them to expect by their own good but limited being. *Homo non proprie humanus sed superhumanus est* [Man is not properly human but superhuman]. This "elevated" condition, however, was not "due" to man or angel but was given in order that the primary end of creation be realized.

The cosmos finds its purpose through its relation to the initial design of God in inviting rational beings to participate in His inner, Trinitarian life. Even though the cosmos comes first in time, it does not come first in the divine intention. God could not simply associate free beings with Himself apart from their free being. Moreover, as Plato said in the *Symposium*, the universe seemed to need, for its own perfection, free creatures who could appreciate it. But the free creature can reject that for which it exists.

The Fall is the account of free creatures claiming to be themselves the cause of the order and nature of things. The essential temptation is to call oneself, and not God, the cause of the distinction between good and evil. To avoid this unpleasant possibility, God's only choice would be not to create at all, so that nothing but God would exist. As such, this would not be a bad thing. God would commit no evil in not creating. Yet, something in the goodness of God seeks to diffuse itself—not of necessity but out of delight. This aspect of goodness lies at the origin of our being, and at the origin of creation.

Evidently, the First Parents, like the angels, were themselves intended for God's initial purpose in creation. They were not simply "natural" human beings. Had they definitively not sinned, their destiny would have been the elevated relation to the inner life of God that is promised to all rational creation. We do not know how this would have worked. What changed with the Fall was not the ultimate end for which human beings were created, but rather the means whereby—granted their free rejection of God's initial plan—this end could be achieved.

Revelation, through the promises to Israel and the Incarnation, and through both to all the nations, did not change the end for which God created in the first place. But man would be saved, as even the Greeks suspected, by suffering. The Incarnation and Redemption restored to man a way of reaching the original end for which he was created. The Redemption did not, however, restore the elevated gifts—especially that of not dying—that were given to the original free human beings.

Of course, God understood that the Fall would happen, but His knowing did not cause it. Rather, the cause lies in the will and love of the free creature. The Incarnation and Redemption, the Cross and Resurrection, are the way that human beings are now to return to God's initial purpose. The Incarnation is the surprising, almost shocking response of God to our freedom. We would like, perhaps, to think of some "gentler" way. But the particular Incarnation and Redemption that we know in revelation teaches us both the terrible consequences of sin and the extraordinary free glory into which we are invited in fulfilling God's initial purpose.

The original plan of God in creation is being worked out in history, and our unique lives are immersed in this very working out. The most important thing in history is that we achieve the end for which we are created. This end is offered to everyone and, as John Paul II often says, God does not deny the means for those of good will who seek. But this possibility is dependent on the Incarnation and the Redemption through Church and sacrament that Christ has revealed to be the way back to our end. This end is to live eternally, while beholding and delighting in the inner life of God in the company of all beings who choose to accept this end, an acceptance that no one can achieve without grace and personal choice.

❧

CHAPTER 10

A Last Lecture:
On Essays and Letters

I

MAURICE BARING, the English diplomat and author, once wrote a book entitled *Lost Lectures.* I was once asked to take part in an undergraduate lecture series under the rubric "Last Lectures." What is it, asked the series organizers, that one would say were this to be the last lecture of one's days? Clearly, this brings up in another way the unseriousness of human affairs we have considered in these pages. We would want our "last" lecture to be "serious," but only in the sense that it pointed to the highest things and to our place within them. A designation as the "last lecture" imbues the subject matter with a certain solemnity, whether we think of the "last lecture" of one's life or the "last lecture" of one's academic days. We naturally suppose that anyone would want, on such an occasion, to leave something lasting, something profound, something altogether serious, though not neglecting the delight of being and the amusement of our lot.

We assume, do we not, that human lives mean something? Do we not maintain that we can formulate this meaning in words for others to read and ponder down the ages? I was recently at the Lincoln Memorial. On its left wall, the reader will recall, is written in stone the Gettysburg Address. "The world will little note, nor long remember what we say here...," Lincoln laconically wrote on his envelope that day. However, contrary to Lincoln's prophecy, without those words we would probably have forgotten "what they did here." Indeed, the vivid articulation of being in words is itself a part of *what is.* The Word was made flesh. And every day we seek to endow our flesh with words.

We can also recall the final address of Socrates to the jury of Athenian citizens who had just condemned him to death. On hearing the verdict—a verdict that always surprises us, though it shouldn't—Socrates turned to the jury. His playful mood suddenly ceased. Socrates assured them that for the rest of history, they would each be infamous. For whenever in the future anyone might read the account of his death, those who voted to execute him would be ingloriously remembered as those who killed the philosopher. That vote would characterize their unfortunate presence in this world.

The human race knows of the death of Socrates because of a short dialogue written by a young man who at the time of his writing was not much older than ordinary undergraduates. Plato tells us that Socrates had reflected further on something besides the future reputation of the Athenian jurors. He explained to his accusers what they had done: "For I go to die and you remain to live," he told them finally, "but who has the better part is known only to God" (*Apology,* 42). To choose to live unjustly, he had already explained to them, was not worthy of anyone. These are, of course, solemn words, befitting the occasion, as words are supposed to do, to recall Lincoln.

What I want to discuss here is something perhaps different, perhaps less solemn, though perhaps not. What I want to suggest is the importance of letters and essays in our lives. What I mean by letters are those written pages sent to someone we may or may not know personally, something ordinarily posted, and something that takes time to arrive at its destination. By essays, I mean short or relatively short accounts of almost anything, including the accounts of men and women about all the things that occur in the lives of human beings, things ranging from God to the smallest and most ephemeral of things—the rock we found on the beach at Santa Cruz, or the corner we turned on a street in Rome.

II

We live in a world, of course, increasingly ruled by e-mail, instant communication, video, satellites, wireless phones. We have at our fingertips, increasingly, everything ever written, ever sung, ever spoken, ever acted. We begin to wonder: Is it all equally important? Will we find wisdom amidst this endless stream of information? In a way, I think, letters and essays may save us simply because they do preserve, in the immediacy of their address and style, the particularity of things, without the knowledge of which there is no wisdom.

In a sense, nothing I will say here necessarily denigrates these newer communication forms, except perhaps for my mood in discussing them. I am, in fact, a diligent "e-mailer" myself. But I am mindful of the beginning of the Third Part of Cicero's *De Officiis*, where he cites the famous passage about his "never being less alone than when he is alone." A certain unexpected strength lies behind this remark. Being alone is the condition, ultimately, of not being alone. Wisdom and information are not the same thing. We need a certain space, a certain lapse of time in which we are alone—actively alone in that "never less alone" sense that Cicero set down for us.

But what did Cicero mean, precisely, about "never being less idle than when he was alone and never less lonely than when he was by himself"? These words, do not forget, were recorded by a man who wrote one of the very best essays ever composed on the subject of friendship, *De Amicitia*, leaving us to wonder if some relationship exists between being able to be alone with the highest things and being able to have friends. This is a theme developed in another way by Aristotle in the last three books of the *Ethics*, among other places.

We still hear, even in our own lives, words like "solitude" or "contemplation." And the modern concept of "loneliness," the condition of being alone with no friends even in the midst of large cities, the "lonely crowd," seems almost the opposite of what Cicero was getting at when he spoke of being alone. Students are, mostly, young enough not to have fully realized what solitude and contemplation might ultimately mean. Yet it must be insisted that the quality of our interior lives is the first thing that is important about our relationship with others, including God. And this interior life can only be freely given and freely received. It exists in no other way.

Cicero, moreover, was one of the world's greatest letter writers and essayists. And this is what I want to talk about, the importance of short essays and letters in our lives. Above all reading matter, and above all writing matter, I myself love the essay and the letter. I do not wish to disdain or neglect the treatise, the long book, the novel, the poem, nor even less the other arts—painting, sculpture, and especially music. But I love a book of essays or a book of letters.

III

I have always found something particularly wonderful in essays and collections of letters, as well as in individual letters written to me. I look forward to receiving a letter I can actually "answer." Yet whether we can "answer" any letter we receive depends obviously on the arrival of the letter itself. We must await that. Waiting is part of the reading. But the fact is that we seldom receive the letters we "expect," and often the ones we do not expect are the best ones we ever receive. The essays that charm us most are often ones we come upon by chance wandering through an old library on a rainy day, or by a random reading of an essay in the book shelved next to the one we were searching for. In my "last lecture," I would want at least to suggest, in the beginning, a favorite letter and a favorite short essay of mine, things that made me pause and look at them again and again, though few probably ever heard of them before.

The first is a letter of Flannery O'Connor to Louise Abbott in 1959; the second, a wonderful essay of Hilaire Belloc entitled, "On Unknown People."[1] I will let the reader find them at his leisure. He will be very pleased by them, though somewhat upset too. But I will cite at least a sentence from each. "I think there is no suffering greater," Flannery O'Connor wrote in her letter, "than what is caused by the doubts of those who would believe." "Who carved the wood in St. James's Church at Antwerp?" Belloc asks in his essay. "I think the name is known for part of it, but no one did the whole or anything like the whole, and yet it is all one thing."

Several years ago I wrote an essay entitled "Letters and the Spiritual Life." Let me cite, if I may, some lines from that essay, as they give some of the spirit of what I want to say here:

> The letter comes unexpectedly some morning or afternoon in the post. It bears that element of surprise, which is almost the deepest of our spiritual concepts. We can read a letter, read it again, set it aside, answer it in a week or a month or, sometimes, not at all. And even though we can now tape phone calls, and ultimately, I suppose, phono-vision calls—God forbid!—nobody really thinks of re-listening to a phone conversation just as we re-read a letter. There is a profound reason for this, I think. For the phone makes us "present" in a way, while a letter reaches rather our privacy, our aloneness. And this is where we are most ourselves, most protected from the blare and glare of the world that tempts our vanity and engulfs our meek and half-hearted efforts to be good.[2]

I would now add to this reflection a paradox; that is, because we want what we receive to be free, we must not anticipate too much that our best letters will be answered, even though we want them to be. Letters are a "cor-respondence," things that invite, even await, a response. But if the word sent to us is not freely sent, we cannot expect it to be what we really want. Answers and responses can come to us in many ways, not always by the post. Letters are part of our wholeness.

We should not forget also that St. Paul's writings are called letters—"epistles"—as are several other parts of the New Testament. We cannot help but be touched, I think, when we come to the end of, say, the Second Letter of John. There he says, "I have much to write to you, but I do not care to put it down in black and white. But I hope to visit you and talk with you face to face, so that our joy may be complete. The children of your Sister, chosen by God, send their greetings."

If we reflect on that passage from John, we can see that letters are always particular. I am not here so much talking of business letters but of letters we send to someone, to some specific place. The letter is unique because, in its purest form, it deals with the person to whom we send it and with his or her relation to us. Yet it includes somehow all that is known or even knowable, for that is precisely what we have in common, the great truths and the insignificant deeds of our lives, our lot, and our world. Letters always will leave much to be said, as John implied. And I should think that, often, we can say things in letters that we are reluctant to say directly, for better or worse. Serious letters are never, in this sense, simply neutral. John is right. We do hope to visit, to see the person to whom we write, to "talk to him face to face." The letter is a claim against time and distance.

In both the Old and New Testament, we notice that the peculiar longing we have for God is precisely to see Him "face to face," an expression we find in St. Paul. If I can put it this way, a letter is what we do when we cannot see someone face to face. Thus, a letter is also a preparation to see face to face, something that requires not just sight, but inner sight. And this inner sight depends on our affirming with Cicero that we are never less alone than when we are alone. Paul said that our joy is not complete until we see face to face. That too is a remarkable insight. Joy, as Josef Pieper remarked, is "having what we love."[3] So there continues to be, I am convinced, something of a solemnity, the solemnity of anticipated joy, about good letters.

IV

The difference between a letter and an essay is, in one sense, not very great; in another sense it is infinite. In preparing this "last lecture," I asked a friend what the difference is between an essay and a letter. She answered, with remarkable acuity, "the difference between two and three hundred." That answer recalls a remark of Chesterton that there is more difference between two and three than between three and three million. The letter is written to one person; the essay is written for everyone.

Letters and essays are both short "efforts" as the French word *essayer* ("to try") implies. Even long letters verge on essays in that they begin to reflect on the truth of things. In fact, in the eighteenth century, letters and essays were often the same, as letters were intended to be circulated.

I think of my favorite essays—Hazlitt's "On Going a Journey," Samuel Johnson's *Idler* and *Rambler* essays, Stevenson's "Walking Tours," Belloc's "Jane Austen," Dorothy Sayers's "The Greatest Drama Ever Staged," Montaigne's "On Solitude," Cicero's "On Old Age," C. S. Lewis's "The Weight of Glory," Chesterton's "A Defense of Rash Vows," and Russell Kirk's "The Valley of the Shadow of Books." There are the delightful essays of P. J. O'Rourke, Florence King, and Joseph Epstein, to all of whom my friend and former student Scott Walter introduced me, and of course there are a thousand others. In essays and letters, it is perfectly alright to have our favorites.

The essay differs from the letter, as I have suggested, because the essay is directed to everyone—to the three hundred or three million, but not to a someone. To the friend we know and love, we want to spell out everything, but there is something radically particular about this spelling out, something finite and directed. We are making all our world known to a someone, not making everyone aware of what he did not know. To the reader of our essays, we have no personal relation, at least not until someone writes to us about them. We do not know who, if anyone, might read them.

Letters, again, can come from anyone, from people we do not know. I frequently get letters from readers I have never met, and sometimes I am moved to write an essayist I do not know. Indeed, after a while, we can become friends with people to whom we write. We eventually even may meet some of them, at which time we find that though they do not look anything like we thought, we somehow know their souls from their letters.

An essay has a special freedom about it. Its subject matter is literally unlimited. We can write about anything. Chesterton once wrote an essay on "chasing his hat." We can write about places, time, friends, love, hatred, God, politics, our aches and pains, our thoughts, our deeds, our delights, our sorrows, even our boring sins. The essay is a place for wit, for seriousness, for "wasting our time," which is what we should do with our friends, as the Little Prince said. And there is also something of Luther's "here I stand" about an essay, I think.

Thus, when we come to books of essays, we can find almost anything. There is a great wonder about what we can read in a few short pages. I recently re-read Etienne Gilson's "The Future of Augustinian Metaphysics," a title that is no doubt daunting, yet it is one of the great essays I have ever read, one well worth reading again and again. I also think of Art Buchwald, who comes up with mad titles like "Gun Stamps for the Poor" and "It Isn't Our Fault!" And no one should miss James Thurber's poignant *My Life and Hard Times.*

V

Letters and essays—I speak of them both as things to be written and things to be read. I suppose that letters, for most of us, will be more a part of our actual writing lives than essays, though when it comes to reading, we may well read many more essays than we shall ever write. But letters also sometimes are published. I think of the letters in Boswell's *Life of Samuel Johnson,* or Isak Dinesen's *Letters from Africa,* or Jane Austen's *Selected Letters: 1796-1817,* all of which I am fortunate enough to be familiar with.

The letter and essay will be, for most of us, the only recorded mark of our existence, the only way in which words will be put to our being. It is true that we can record on film or disk all sorts of incidents, from marriages to graduations to parties to speeches. And yet, if we take a family photo album and look through it, we will wonder just what our grandfather or great-aunt Harriet really thought about things. Unless we have some record—some letter, some essay, something they wrote—we will know very little about them. I have already received the last letter I will ever receive from my brother Jack, who died in 1995. He was a good letter writer.

We actually live in a time when the physical record of our existence is disappearing. Cremation is replacing burial, so that ashes are now mostly scattered. My Uncle Jim was to be spread over a golf course in Florida. There are no monuments or tombstones to mark the burial places of most of the individuals who have ever lived. And indeed, paper rots and electronic equipment deteriorates or becomes obsolete, so that there is an enormous cultural and technical problem in preserving words as well as stones and photos. If someone goes to the cemetery in the Episcopal churchyard in Alexandria, Virginia, he will see the fading chiseling on the tombstones. All finite things fade, not just ourselves.

In conclusion, then, in my last lecture I would want to record something important about our lives. Essays keep us alert to the wonder of things in a way that nothing else does. Letters keep us in touch when we are not literally before those with whom we would see face to face. We are never less alone than when we discover an essay we never saw before, or when we receive an unexpected letter some morning when we thought we were by ourselves.

In reading letters and essays, we remain by ourselves, but we become alive. Our idleness passes into leisure, into the activity of reflection, wonder, and contemplation. As Jane Austen wrote to her sister Cassandra on April 21, 1805, "I am much obliged to you for writing to me again so soon; your letter yesterday was quite an unexpected pleasure." This is it, isn't it? The unexpected pleasures that come to us from nowhere and inform us about everything in the lives of those we love, of those we know, and of those whom we would know.

❦

CHAPTER 11

Philosophy: Why What Is Useless Is the Best Thing about Us

Intelligence [*phronesis, prudentia*] does not control wisdom or the better part of the soul, just as medical science does not control health. For it does not use health, but only aims to bring health into being; hence it prescribes for the sake of health but does not prescribe to health. Besides, saying that intelligence controls wisdom would be like saying that political science rules the gods because it prescribes about everything in the city.

— ARISTOTLE, *Nicomachean Ethics*

Dissipation: The mother of dissipation is not joy but joylessness.

— NIETZSCHE, "Mixed Opinions and Maxims"

I

LET ME BEGIN with a sentence found early in Cicero's *De Senectute*: "No praise, then, is too great for philosophy!" These are words that shall guide our reflections here. However, we shall mean by philosophy not just the moral philosophy that Cicero praised, nor merely political philosophy, which wonders how to render the forceful politician benevolent to the truths of the theoretic life, but philosophy as such, the philosophy that includes metaphysics as well as moral and political philosophy. I maintain that philosophy as such is "useless"; I also maintain that it is the best thing about us, for it leads to the highest things, to things perhaps beyond philosophy but not unrelated to its most perceptive inquiries. In short, there are things "worth doing for their own sakes," as the Greeks taught us with surprising precision.

The choice of modern man, it is said in a famous book, is between Aristotle and Nietzsche.[1] The wit of Nietzsche makes the choice of Aristotle quite sensible, though the philosophy of Aristotle, since it requires discipline and virtue, makes the dire conclusions of Nietzsche seem almost inevitable. So it is not totally arbitrary that I begin these thoughts on philosophy with two brief citations, one from Aristotle and one from Nietzsche. At first sight, neither passage will seem to direct itself to the stated title and subtitle of this chapter, to philosophy or what is best about us. Aristotle talks of prudence, health, and the gods; Nietzsche notices an ironic connection between dissipation and joy, or better, joylessness.

We are all most interested in both health and joy, though perhaps not for the same reasons. Even if we are not healthy, we certainly desire to be so. Even if we be joyless, we want to know joy; otherwise we would not suspect that we lacked it. Indeed, if we are dissipated, we probably, at some point, long for order in our lives. And suffering, which implies the lack of health and perhaps of joy, is not, in the ultimate order of things, totally without purpose. "Is it better to suffer evil or to do it?" is a very ancient and hardly indifferent question found authoritatively answered in the *Apology* of Socrates. Even if it is better to suffer evil than to do it, we still do not seek to encourage the existence of the evil just so we can suffer. Suffering evil, though we are reluctant to admit it, may indeed be evil's ultimate remedy. Isaiah's "Suffering Servant" remains both mysterious and instructive in this light. "Man learns by suffering," the Greek poet observed. And what does he learn? Surely he learns that just as the purpose of war is peace, so the purpose of suffering is health, even beatitude, the highest activity of health.

Aristotle's rather enigmatic observation in the *Ethics* that medical science prescribes for the sake of health but not *to* health contains one of the most fertile insights in all of philosophy (1145a10). For it says nothing less than that when we have our health, "health produces health," as he put it in another place (1144a5). That is, once a doctor has helped to cure us (ultimately, nature cures us), once we are healthy, the doctor's task ends. *Qua* doctor, he can tell us no more. The question then arises, "Now what?" What do we "do" when we are healthy, when we are no longer concerned about our health and how to recover or preserve it? When we are not confined to a hospital, what is to occupy us? If we are made to be healthy, what is the activity of health? What is the life of "health" that "health" produces? It must be more than just keeping our health. For starters, St. Thomas points out in his *Commentary on Aristotle's Nicomachean Ethics* that "proper adaptation to [human] affairs and people is more laborious and difficult than knowing remedies in which the whole art of medicine consists" (1075).

When we are healthy, we do not notice the functioning of our various powers and capacities; we are externally oriented, noticing what it is that fascinates or interests us. Does man, then, have a peculiar activity that sets him apart, something he delights in just doing? And if he does, would this delightful activity be merely an unintended accident? Is his given being complete without the activity that follows on what he is? "Do the carpenter and the leather-worker have their functions and actions, while a human being has none, and is by nature idle (in vain), without function?" Aristotle asks. "Or just as an eye, hand, foot and, in general, every bodily part apparently has a function, may we likewise ascribe to a human being some function besides all these?" (*Ethics*, 1097b28–33). And if there is such a function, is it best to be described as "necessary" or "useful"? Necessary always points to the unnecessary. The useful always points to what is beyond use. The part points to the whole. Our hand, the ultimate tool in the universe, that "part" by which our mind gets outside of mind to change things, is not a hand if it is not attached to us, as Aristotle also remarked.

The Little Prince, I noted earlier, said that it is the time that we "waste" with our friends that really counts. Is the world so occupied that we have no time to waste? Why do we like to play and to watch others playing? Plato said that human life is not "serious." Man is the "play-thing" of the gods (*Laws*, 803c). In saying this he was not denigrating us, but praising our lives for what they are. It is not "necessary" that we exist. Yet, we do exist. We exist for a reason not rooted in determinism. The fact that we exist but need not exist expresses the most profound thing about us. It implies that we exist because of a choice, a love, a freedom grounded in what is beyond necessity. It implies that our lives should reflect this non-necessity, this freedom to be recipients of goods and graces of which we are not the cause.

Aristotle told us not to listen to those who tell us that, being human, we should devote our lives to human things (*Ethics*, 1177b32–78a2). Such "human" things are political things, economic things, things that seem to take all of our time, things that have their place in the order of reality yet do not describe what we are really about. It is all right to spend much time on political and economic things, for it is permitted to be what we are: finite, mortal beings. As Aristotle noted, if man were the highest being in the universe, these human and political things would constitute the highest science (*Ethics*, 1141a20–22). But man is not the highest being in the universe. Political science does not "rule the gods," as our intro-ductory citation reminds us. Aristotle tells us to spend as much time as we can on the highest things, even if the knowledge we acquire is little by comparison. To be human we must be more than human, a truth that we are often loath to accept.

Aristotle called our capacity to contemplate the highest things pre-cisely "divine," even while he was sure that we are not gods and should not want to become gods. When we think about friendship, we do not want to cease to be what we are. We don't want our friend to become a king or a god (*Ethics*, 1159a5–11). But we still are tempted to be as gods, to make political science the highest science, to claim that the whole order of things, especially human things, falls under the power of our deliberative choice. If we are to have an activity that is called "divine," it must always remain under the light of what we are. The highest things, including ourselves, are given to us; we do not make them to be what they are.

II

Though we are sometimes told—and sometimes tell ourselves—that joy will result from dissipation, it never quite does. Even Nietzsche warns us. We can take the truth of this observation about dissipation on faith, on the testimony of others, or we can test it ourselves, as I believe the young Augustine did. The results are the same. "Do not envy those who do evil," one of the Psalms cautions us. We find that the rather cynical but perceptive Nietzsche is quite right. Plato talked of a kind of "divine madness," as if to say that our senses and our minds are not given solely for their own exercise but to hear and see, to be wholly absorbed by, what is not ourselves, to hear and see *what is*. Nietzsche's word, "joylessness," is one I find to be remarkably provocative, as he intended it to be. "You will not find what you are looking for," he implies, "if you look for it in dissipation." Here, he too is on the side of the gods. But what are we looking for? For we do look and seek, even if we deny that we do.

"I find students are frequently flabbergasted, especially those who are agnostics," Eric Voegelin tells us,

> when I tell them that they all act, whether agnostic or not, as if they were immortal. Only under the assumption of immortality, of fulfill-ment beyond this life, is the seriousness of action intelligible which they actually put into their work and which has a fulfillment nowhere in this life however long they may live. They all act as if their lives made sense immortally, even if they deny immortality, deny the existence of

a psyche, deny the existence of a Divinity—in brief, if they are just the sort of fairly corrupt average agnostics that you find among college students today. One shouldn't take their agnosticism too seriously, because they act as if in fact they weren't agnostics.[2]

Basic principles operate in us even when we deny their existence. It is safer to watch what someone does rather than to listen to what he says.

To declare our absolute liberty, or to refuse to observe the Commandments or to practice the virtues, may often seem positively "romantic." We delight in being "rebels" with, or even without, a cause. But it is Nietzsche—not the clergy, and not even Aristotle—who told us that "God is dead, and we have killed him," and who alerts us to the moral dangers that accompany this posture. On the basis of our voluntary murder of God in our souls, Nietzsche tells us to be free—or rather, tells us that we are condemned to be free. But in our absolute freedom, we still know dissipation, a rather dull, repetitive life, in fact, as St. Thomas implied in a famous passage (ST, I-II, 91, 6). However, if contrary to Nietzsche, God is *not* dead, is it still possible to hope that joy is open to us even when we discover that our ways do not produce it, when we discover in fact that we ourselves produce the evils that cause others to suffer, that lead them to the joylessness of dissipation?

We can conceive the divinity in terms of mercy and not merely justice. Justice—the terrible virtue, as I call it—may not be the last word in the universe. Perhaps, as St. Thomas implied, the world is not created in justice (ST, I, 21, 4). Knowing ourselves, we may well hope that it isn't. But if God is indeed dead, little is left to us but despair. Nietzsche tells the truth, in his own way. For many moderns, his testimony is more credible than that of God Himself. For, ironically, God too promised joylessness as the result of dissipation. Nietzsche's biting aphorisms often inadvertently—or, I sometimes think, intentionally—rediscover and point to a lost Christianity. Nietzsche's main complaint about the Last Christian, the one who died on the Cross, was that His followers, judging by their actions, did not believe in Him. About a century after the death of Nietzsche, when the Pope visited St. Louis, the American media was fond of ferreting out famous and ordinary Catholics who affirmed before the world that they "disagreed" with the Pope about how to live. They confirmed Nietzsche in his estimate about the weakness of faith. But the content of what was originally believed and originally revealed is better than anything that we can concoct for ourselves. This is the judgment under which modernity lives.

III

Josef Pieper remarked that "joy is a by-product." He meant by this curious observation that we cannot make joy an object of our choice or even of our intellect. It is not another "thing," nor is it, like health, something a medical practitioner can restore. We can perhaps recognize it when we have it, but we cannot buy it, demand it, or claim a right for it. It seems to belong to that category of things that must be "given" to us. We must be the sort of people capable of receiving gifts. Contrary to our Declaration, we do not have a "right" to happiness, or even its pursuit. Who would enforce that right? Is our happiness "due" to us in justice, or does it come from some other, higher source? Who would develop a public policy to obtain this happiness? Who would define it? What would we be pursuing? We can only deliberate, as Aristotle says, about what we might bring about by our own purposeful actions (*Ethics*, 1112a20–32). We are quite sure that we want to be happy, that we do all we do in order to be happy. Likewise, we want to be joyful. But where happiness is an activity, joy is a kind of receptivity. The latter follows from the former, and the former depends on our doing what is virtuous, what is right. For as Pieper says, joy is the receiving and possessing of what we love; it is not something that we can command or demand. We may never possess what we love and consequently we may never be full of joy. But if we love nothing, no joy is possible.

John Paul II made an unexpected remark in *Fides et Ratio* when he said that, in truth, everyone is a philosopher (#30). I presume he did not intend to denigrate philosophy departments, let alone the diligent philosopher who goes it alone, as all must at some point. He only intended to affirm that it is possible for everyone to know the truth—a very Aristotelian remark, in a way. The Philosopher himself recognized, that since we are all in immediate contact with being, with *what is*, it is possible for ordinary folks to see the truth of things, even if they may not exactly be able to explain what they see in complicated or technical language (*Ethics*, 1180b17–20). We may therefore conclude that joy and happiness are not to be conceived merely as something open to a few, to the philosophers. Nor was it the philosophers who made us most aware that *what is* is open to everyone.

Yet, I am here to praise the philosopher. After all, it was Aristotle, the Philosopher, who remarked, in a touching passage, that "we can do fine actions even if we do not rule earth and sea; for even from moderate resources we can do actions expressing virtue. This is evident to see, since many private citizens seem to do decent actions no less than people in power do—even more, in fact.... The life of someone whose activity expresses virtue will be happy" (*Ethics*, 1179a4–9). In a declining, corrupt but prosperous civil society, this may well be our only charter of freedom, our only avenue to both joy and happiness. The initial battles, I think, are not fought in the public forum or in the wars of the world, but in the hearts of men, especially in the hearts and minds of the dons, the intellectual and clerical dons. We all need enough philosophy to give us a chance to estimate erring intellectuals.

IV

Charlie Brown is lying on his back with his head propped on a stone for a pillow. Lucy is looking at him in this prone position with some confusion. Charlie says to her, "If I tell you something, Lucy, will you promise not to laugh?" Naturally, she replies, "I promise." In the next scene, Charlie, still on his back, tells her earnestly that "this is very personal, and I don't want you to laugh." "You have my solemn promise," she assures him. In the third frame, Charlie explains his concern: "Sometimes, I lie awake at night listening for a voice that will cry, 'We *like* you, Charlie Brown!'" In the fourth scene, all we see is Charlie flipped over on his head, while Lucy, with not a thought of her solemn promises, screams in utter delight at the absurdity of this nightly voice, "Ha, Ha, Ha, Ha!"[3] Charlie Brown voices not only the desire to be taken seriously, but also the fear that it is all rather silly, these highest things, this desire to be loved, to know joy.

Aristotle discovered in us human beings, besides the fact that we are rational and political animals, that we are also *homines risibiles.* We are the beings who laugh—and perhaps, recalling Lucy and Charlie Brown, the beings who are laughed at. Aristotle also reminded us that there is a time and place for laughter. The buffoon who laughs at everything and everybody is not a charming character, nor is the somber man who laughs at nothing (*Ethics*, 1128a34–b5). Aristotle also noticed that the ability to laugh is a sign of metaphysical intelligence. He realized that our laughter results from our ability to see the relationships, or lack thereof, among things. And the ability to see relations is the first requirement of the metaphysician. When we laugh, too, we see that what is put side by side does not go together, or that what is not in proximity ought to be joined. And we cannot help but thinking that this capacity for laughter is connected to our joy.

Chesterton's profound remark that the one thing that the Son of God did not show us while He was on earth was His "mirth" did not presume that the Lord did not know mirth.[4] Indeed, it was Chesterton's view that the sort of joy for which we are made is so much more delightful than anything we can know, even by analogy, that it would only depress us if we were to see it before we were really prepared. The real crisis of our being, if we would only reflect on it, is that we are given too much, not too little, that we are made for a joy we are tempted to reject because we cannot imagine it. The structure of the present human world might well be seen as the result of the rejection of a gift, which is not due us.

The world is replete with attempts of our own imaginings, disguised as philosophy, to replace what was intended to be our gift and our joy. Philosophy suggests that what is best about us is what is "useless." At first, it sounds odd to argue that what is best in us is useless and that this "what is best" is, indeed, philosophy. Philosophy, we know, means that we love and seek wisdom, the order and content of the highest things. Philosophy is not merely a knowledge but a way of life, a commitment to what is true. Likewise, Socrates told us that philosophy is a preparation for death. He chided the young followers in his cell on his last day for weeping. Socrates admonished them because their weeping was a sign that they did not understand what he had been trying to teach them. Yet, we cannot but sympathize with the tears of these potential philosophers.

V

What is best in us is "useless." I want to approach this enigmatic proposition by way of pleasure. To say that what is best in us is "useless" does not mean that what is best in us does not have its own proper pleasure. Samuel Johnson, I think, had it right. On April 15, 1778, Boswell records a remark of Johnson concerning the famous thesis of Mandeville that our vices cause our wealth. Echoing Aristotle, Johnson remarks that

> Pleasure of itself is not a vice. Having a garden, which we all know to be perfectly innocent, is a great pleasure. At the same time, in this state of being there are many pleasures [that are] vices, which however are so immediately agreeable that we can hardly abstain from them. The happiness of Heaven will be, that pleasure and virtue will be perfectly consistent.[5]

Heaven is not a place in which pleasures are lacking, but a place in which their true reality is seen in the acts for which they are intended.

Aristotle made the same point in another way. He acknowledged that for every activity there is a proper pleasure, so that if a pleasure is wrong, it is not because it is pleasurable but because the activity in which it exists as a "bloom" or perfection is wrong. He added that there are many activities that we would "be eager for even if they brought no pleasure, e.g., seeing, remembering, knowledge, having the virtues" (*Ethics*, 1174a4–5). Aristotle also says that having the virtues is itself necessary for knowing reality as it is; otherwise we end up using our knowledge to pursue ends that are not the highest (*Ethics*, 1178a16–20). But though knowledge is among the things that Aristotle mentioned we would want even if there were no proper pleasure attached, there *is* a proper pleasure attached to knowledge, a pleasure that makes the activity even more delightful, even more absorbing.

The degree of pleasure varies according to the act. If we do not experience the highest pleasures, it is quite likely that we will lapse into what are called lower ones, that is, into activities that are disordered, separating their purpose from the pleasure connected with them. Aristotle is remarkably certain that those who experience the highest things are not usually those with great wealth or political power. "For virtue and understanding, the sources of excellent activities, do not depend on holding supreme power," he wrote. "Further, these powerful people have had no taste of pure and civilized pleasure, and so they resort to bodily pleasures" (*Ethics*, 1176b19–21). Politicians, those "holding supreme power," resort to bodily pleasures not because they are busy about political things but because their souls have no taste for "pure and civilized pleasure." It is difficult for a politician to have a contemplative life, but without it, he is in danger of undermining even the political life. Aristotle was quite aware that the political life stood in a very precarious moral position. It could not satisfy our souls through its own pleasures, by the honor due it. A confusion about the relative importance of the political life, the highest of the practical sciences but not the highest life as such, could well leave empty the soul that lacked a taste for the higher things, a soul that lacked philosophy.

Aristotle frequently speaks of things that are worth doing "for their own sakes." Not everything can be done "in order to" do something else. That is, ultimately, there must be something that is just worth doing, something that at the same time is ours and takes us outside of ourselves. Notice that Aristotle said that the politicians who lacked a "taste for pure and civilized pleasure" not only have no inner resources whereby they might see the limitations of power, but, lacking this higher pleasure, lapse into what Aristotle calls "bodily pleasures." They are less than complete. The highest things give rise to the highest pleasures. If we do not know them, we blind ourselves.

This passage recalls Plato's discussion of the tyrant, especially Alcibiades or Callicles, both of whom are pictured as attractive, shrewd, and powerful politicians. For Plato and Aristotle, the tyrant charmed the people. The tyrant knew citizens' souls, fearing only those with inner virtue, and paid close attention to the people's wants, whatever they were. What is also characteristic of both Alcibiades and Callicles, of tyrants in general, is that they have no inner soul, no order of virtue. Callicles said that he studied philosophy in college but gave it up as dangerous because it got in his way in politics. Machiavelli was later to say substantially the same thing. Alcibiades ends up betraying Athens and seeks, unsuccessfully, to subvert Socrates, the philosopher. Both Alcibiades and Callicles admit that they take their norms not from inner principles of *what is*, but from what the people want. This shifting criterion implies that the tyrant wants to use the people for his own ends. And these ends are never those of the self-sufficient contemplative, never those that give rise to the kind of pure and civilized pleasure that indicates a soul aware of the attraction of the highest things.

VI

To make this point in another way, let me recount the first letter in the *Correspondence of Shelby Foote & Walker Percy.* The letter is dated May Day, 1948, from Foote to Percy. Foote is discussing what is involved in learning to write. To learn to write, Foote tells Percy, one has to be an apprentice for five or more years. One has to write, rewrite, tear up, and write again. He adds, but the most heart-breaking thing about [writing] is [this]: the better you get, the harder you will have to work—because your standards will rise with your ability. I mentioned "work"—it is the wrong word: because if you're serious, the whole creative process is attended with pleasure, in a form which very few people ever know. Putting two words together in a sequence that pleases you, really *pleases* you, brings a satisfaction which must be kin to what a businessman feels when he manages a sharp transaction—something like that but on a higher plane because the businessman must know that soon he will have spent the dollars he made, but these two words which the writer set together have produced an effect which will never die as long as men can read with understanding.[6]

The human creative process has its own pleasure which resides in the work and almost ceases to be work, passing into contemplation itself, into the "effect which will never die as long as men can read with understanding."

Before the 1999 Super Bowl, the *Washington Post* ran a long feature article on Bill Romanowski, the Denver Broncos' tough and controversial linebacker. Romanowski is portrayed as a man who likes to play all the time, who would play both offense and defense if possible, who plays hard and does not count the injuries, "a throwback to the days when football players considered blood stains on their jerseys and a mouth full of cracked teeth to be a badge of honor." Romanowski is then quoted as saying, in a line that I want to reflect on here in the context of doing things for their own sakes, "I'm a guy who plays every play like its his last.... They say if you love what you do, you don't have to work a day in your life." This wonderful remark gets close to what we mean by leisure and contemplation, to philosophy, to the best thing in us as precisely useless, to things we enjoy doing for their own sakes, even if they mean blood on our jerseys.

We do not have to rule land and sea to lead the contemplative life; indeed, that might be an impediment. Such a life has its own pleasure, pure and civilized, without which we lapse into other pleasures not so innocent or riveting. In Mell Lazarus's cartoon "Miss Peach," we are in a kindergarten. We see a very precocious Francine talking with a much slower Arthur. He asks her, "What are you doing?" "Thinking," she replies. This confuses Arthur: "Thinking?" "Yes," Francine explains pertly, "I'm getting ideas." "Ideas are wonderful," she pronounces. "Ideas? What are ideas?" Arthur persists. "You're kidding. Ideas are, well, 'thoughts.'" "Thoughts?" Arthur repeats confusedly, as if thoughts are new to him. "Yes, things that come into your mind." With this explanation, Arthur is pictured with a question mark over his head. He doesn't get it. "They come into your head," she explains. "What do they look like?" he wants to know. Francine patiently responds, "Arthur, ideas are intangible. They don't look like anything in particular." Arthur still bears the question mark; it makes no sense to him. "Ideas! Ideas!! Haven't you ever had any, Arthur? Wispy things that sort of float in and out of your mind at odd moments?" Francine awaits light in Arthur's eyes, but Arthur continues uncomprehendingly to stare at her. Finally, in the last scene, to a thoroughly disgusted Francine, Arthur brightly replies, "Oh, yes! I've had those! Funny, I've always assumed they were Unidentified Flying Objects!"[7]

Such amusing kindergarten reflections remind us that "thinking" is indeed what we are about—and not just thinking but thinking about reality, about *what is*. Our minds are *capax omnium*, capable of knowing the truth of all things. What fascinates us, what makes us lose track of time and place is the reality that is before us, the reality that we are not. Our minds are given to us so that what is not ourselves can become what we are after the manner of our knowing. It is not sufficient that we simply exist. Human existence includes in some sense the awareness that reality has its own grounding, which we did not give it but about which we are curious, about which we want to know the truth.

"Philosophy strives for knowledge of the whole," Leo Strauss wrote in a famous essay.[8] And in this striving or way of life, in this love of wisdom, philosophy becomes absorbing; it possesses its own pleasure.

We notice nothing of the effort involved in learning. If we love what we do, we do not work. Philosophy, at its best, brings us to questions we cannot fully answer by philosophy. Philosophy brings us a long way. And yet, if we do not attend to philosophy, we will not know the whole that we seek.

Plato, in his *Laws*, asked what it is that we should be about when all things are done. How should we spend our lives? What is beyond us and why is it the best thing about us? We should spend our lives, as this book's title recalls, "singing, sacrificing, and dancing" (803e). We are not the measure but the measured. Therefore, we can have joy, can rejoice in *what is*. About the highest things, we can "do" nothing further than celebrate.

VII

Let me conclude by recalling the title of what is to me the most remarkable book written in recent years. It is called *After Writing: The Liturgical Consummation of Philosophy*, written by an English woman, Catherine Pickstock. The book is a very intricate polemic about the intellectual inadequacies of postmodern thought. It is likewise a book about Plato and a book on the value and limits of writing, a very Platonic theme. Notice that the title refers to the "liturgical" consummation of precisely "philosophy." The book deals with the question that bothered Nietzsche, Strauss, and Voegelin, namely, why is it that modern philosophy so often became an ideology that explained the world not through *what is* but through the constructed ideas of man, the philosopher, who insisted on deriving everything from himself, from, in short, what has come to be called modernity?

Having seen these ideologies in operation, postmodern philosophy protects itself by denying that we can know anything at all. Pickstock's thesis is that philosophy does lead us, especially through Plato, in the right direction, but it needs an ending that philosophy itself can only intimate. The recovery of Plato is essential to our philosophic souls. But notice that she uses the word "consummation"; philosophy itself becomes absorbed in what is beyond itself, in what is already in Plato "useless" because it arouses in us what is more than mere praise. It brings us to what Aristotle called "celebration" (*Ethics*, 1101b30–35).

If I can go back to Nietzsche, the history of modernity is the history of man's celebration of a false reality, a reality that only corresponded to what we ourselves could make for ourselves or impose on our kind. But the discovery of the reality beyond philosophy, or better, to which philosophy points, is not something merely left to us. If we are incapable of finding it by ourselves, we cannot exclude the possibility that it is given to us.

Aristotle, in his treatise on friendship, remarked that it seemed odd that God was lonely, that He lacked what is the highest perfection of human life. The liturgical consummation of philosophy follows from the revelational possibility that God is not alone, that within the divinity there is a completion that includes otherness. The human race and the cosmos itself need not exist in order to alleviate the loneliness of God. And if this is so, we can "do" nothing for God; that is, we are ourselves unnecessary and ultimately "useless," and this is the best thing about us because we can pursue the highest things, the knowledge of the whole, spending our lives "singing, sacrificing, and dancing." Philosophy, our pursuit of truth, is relieved of the burden of our attempt to make the world after our own image. Therefore, joylessness is not our destiny. Joy is the receiving of what we love, even in the highest things. The highest things absorb us, and this is our pleasure; this is why we *are* at all.

Conclusion

BY NOW, the passages and ideas that I dearly love will be evident. I do not tire of citing the Little Prince on "wasting our time" with our friends, nor Aristotle's admonition to not spend all our time on "human" things, nor Eric Voegelin's amusing observation that students treat life as if it were important even though their own philosophic theories do not support this possibility. I like the essay and I like the lecture. I have met many friends through e-mail as well as through letters. I think we can learn something in the universities, but I am also fond of citing E. F. Schumacher's experience that none of the things that were really important were taught in the best university in Christendom when he matriculated there. I remain an advocate of books and authors that very few will ever recommend. I think there is a way to save our souls and a way to save our minds.

Needless to say, I think highly of the philosophic stature of the characters in "Peanuts," as well as those in many other cartoons. I am not surprised to find insights in these sources of surpassing wisdom. I do not hesitate to say so. I am also acquainted with evil, with the poverty and horrors of this world. But I do not find these dire realities an argument against either the world or God. If I have, following Plato, called human life as such "unserious," it is because it is not the most important thing in the world, even to itself. We are sojourners and wayfarers. We look with Madame de Sévigné with a bit of sadness on those places we have loved in our youth, not because they do not remain beautiful, but because we pass on in our lives. We are not destined for this world, even though we may love it. This is the recurrent theme of Chesterton, who said that we are "homesick at home." He often reminded us of God's "mirth," to which we are destined. Yet we cannot bear God's mirth before we are prepared for it.

Boswell speaks of the most exhilarating day of his life, an elegant day. But it is still a day in this particular, given world with friends, conversation, and a certain lightheartedness. Many people who are important in my life, like Boswell, I have never met. Yet, they have taught me many things. I have lived a life of teaching and being taught, the latter before the former. *Contemplata tradere*, as St. Thomas put it, means to pass on the things we have contemplated, but only when we realize that the truth that we have discovered is not ours. Truth is free. We do not possess it as our own private property. We are not less when others share it. Indeed, it is around the truth that our lives and our friendships can flourish.

It is not useless, of course, to know and to contemplate error and evil. We should do so if only to know what they are. It is part of the perfection of our knowing *what is*, that it is, as Plato said, and to know of what is not, that it is not. Leo Strauss said that no one has time in one lifetime to study all the great thinkers. But we need not despair. Many paths lead from something to everything. As Aristotle says, our minds are "capable of all things." Just because we are limited and finite does not mean that the rest of the universe is forever closed to us. The universe that God created was intended to provide for a myriad of independent loci, places from which to view everything and in which everything could, after its own fashion, return and rest.

These activities, these human activities, these "unserious" human activities—teaching, writing, playing, believing, lecturing, philosophizing, singing, dancing—describe how we stand before, and react to, *what is*. If things belong together in an "order," an order of which we ourselves are parts—observing, knowing parts—it is our place in being to know this order, to praise it and wonder about it. We are, as the Greeks called us, "the mortals." We are the beings in the universe who not only will die, but know we will die. And yet, this is not all we know. We know what Socrates told the Athenians—that it is better to die than to do wrong. We know about the doctrine of the resurrection of the body and how it relates to what we would want if we could have it.

If there is any central theme that should be taken away from these reflections, it has to do with joy, with the fact that its existence is more difficult to explain than death, sadness, evil, or finitude. And joy is not to be explained as if it is unknown to the divine source of our being. It is no accident that the greatest of the Christian poems is not called a "tragedy" but a "comedy." We are created in light and for lightsomeness. Plato called us the "playthings" of the gods, not to imply that our lives are frivolous but to make it clear that we are not born in necessity. We are born in the abundance of the Good, in the ordering of that inner life of God that Christians have come to call "the Trinity."

If I have ended these reflections with "philosophy," it is not because I think that philosophy can explain everything. Indeed, some philosophers tell us that we can explain nothing; others tell us that there is nothing to be explained. But it is true that there is a pleasure in walking about Derby and a pleasure in knowing what we can about the highest things. If we visit "the highest things," as I hope these chapters make possible, it is not so that we will be content with how little we can know, but with how much we are given. Philosophy exists, I think, that we might be able to accept what is given beyond what we know. Philosophy as a way of life makes us wonder about ways of life that are not only philosophical. If we are open to *what is*, if we are "eminently teachable," I think, those things we can learn by ourselves and those things that are given to us fall together in an order that accounts for *all that is*.

APPENDIX

These-People-Tell-the-Truth Books

1) *Josef Pieper: An Anthology*

2) G. K. Chesterton, *Orthodoxy*

3) Yves Simon, *A General Theory of Authority*

4) Dorothy Sayers, *The Whimsical Christian*

5) E. F. Schumacher, *A Guide for the Perplexed*

6) Wendell Berry, *Jayber Crow, a Novel*

7) C. S. Lewis, *Mere Christianity*

8) James Boswell, *The Life of Samuel Johnson*

9) Denis de Rougemont, *Love in the Western World*

10) Leon Kass, *The Hungry Soul: Eating and the Perfection of Our Nature*

11) Karol Wojtyla, *Crossing the Threshold of Hope*

12) J. M. Bochenski, *Philosophy: An Introduction*

13) Hilaire Belloc, *The Four Men*

14) Herbert Butterfield, *Christianity and History*

15) Hans Urs von Balthasar, *A Short Primer for Unsettled Laymen*

16) J. R. R. Tolkien, "On Fairy-Stories," *The Tolkien Reader*

17) Julian Simon, *The Ultimate Resource II*

18) Robert Sokolowski, *The God of Faith and Reason*

19) Hadley Arkes, *First Things: An Inquiry into the First Principles of Morals and Justice*

20) Stanley Jaki, *Chance or Reality and Other Essays*

21) Henry Veatch, *Rational Man: A Modern Interpretation of Aristotelian Ethics*

22) Christopher Dawson, *Religion and the Rise of Western Culture*

23) Christopher Derrick, *Escape from Scepticism: Liberal Education as if the Truth Mattered*

24) E. L. Mascall, *The Christian Universe*

25) Peter Kreeft, *Back to Virtue*

Notes

Introduction

1. The lists of books in the Appendix and the Bibliography itself are intended to be not merely records of things cited but directions toward where to go in one's pursuit of the highest things.

2. Leon Kass, *The Hungry Soul: Eating and the Perfection of Our Nature* (Chicago: University of Chicago Press, 1999).

Chapter 1

1. James Boswell, *Life of Johnson* (London: Oxford, 1931), I: 7.

2. Barbara Tuchman, *A Distant Mirror: The Calamitous Fourteenth Century* (New York: Ballantine, 1978), xix.

3. Stanley L. Jaki, *The Road of Science and the Ways to God* (Chicago: University of Chicago Press, 1978).

4. For a Platonic-Christian development of this position, see Catherine Pickstock, *After Writing: The Liturgical Consummation of Philosophy* (Oxford: Blackwell, 1998).

5. *The More Quotable Chesterton*, ed. George Marlin (San Francisco: Ignatius Press, 1988), 478.

Chapter 2

1. Leo Strauss, "What Is Liberal Education?" in *Liberalism: Ancient and Modern* (New York: Basic Books, 1968), 3–8. See also, James V. Schall, S. J., *A Student's Guide to Liberal Learning* (Wilmington, Del.: ISI Books, 2000); *Another Sort of Learning* (San Francisco: Ignatius, 1988).

2. "There is one thing a professor can be absolutely certain of: almost every student entering the university believes, or says he believes, that truth is relative." Allan Bloom, *The Closing of the American Mind* (New York: Simon & Schuster, 1987), 25.

3. Wesley McDonald, "Recovering a Neglected Conservative Mind," *University Bookman* 34, no. 4, (1994): 19–20.

4. Yves Simon, *A General Theory of Authority* (Notre Dame, Ind.: University of Notre Dame Press, 1980), 100.

5. *The Wall Street Journal*, July 24, 1994.

6. Schall, *Another Sort of Learning*. See also Schall, *A Student's Guide to Liberal Learning*.

7. Evelyn Waugh, *Brideshead Revisited* (Boston: Little, Brown, 1945), 9.

8. C. S. Lewis, *The Abolition of Man* (New York: Macmillan, 1947). Peter Kreeft has reformulated Lewis's description in his remarkable *C. S. Lewis for the Third Millennium* (San Francisco: Ignatius Press, 1994).

9. Louis L'Amour, *Education of a Wandering Man* (New York: Bantam, 1990).

10. Wendell Berry, *A Place on Earth*, rev. ed. (New York: North Point, 1983), 11. See also Wendell Berry, *Jayber Crow: The Life Story of Jayber Crow, Barber, of the Port William Membership, as Written by Himself: A Novel* (Washington D.C.: Counterpoint, 2000).

12. Frederick A. Pottle, ed., *Boswell on the Grand Tour: Germany and Switzerland, 1764* (New York: McGraw-Hill, 1953), 133–134.

Chapter 3

1. *Crisis* 8 (September 1990): 16.

2. See James V. Schall, *Does Catholicism Still Exist?* (Staten Island, N.Y.: Alba House, 1994).

3. I call the list "Schall's Unlikely List of Books to Keep Sane By." It can be found in both *Another Sort of Learning* and *A Student's Guide to Liberal Learning*. The list varies. As an appendix to this book, I have included, because of a conversation with Jeremy Beer, a "These-People-Tell-the-Truth" list of books. It is not much different from the "Sane Books" lists.

4. Frederick Wilhelmsen, "Great Books: Enemies of Wisdom?" *Modern Age*, 31 (Summer/Fall, 1987): 323–31.

5. Schall, *Another Sort of Learning*; also Schall, *A Student's Guide to Liberal Learning*; "Books and the Intellectual Life," *Vital Speeches*, LXV (March 1, 1999), 316–20.

6. Mother Teresa, *Love: A Fruit Always in Season: Daily Meditations of Mother Teresa*, ed. Dorothy Hunt (San Francisco: Ignatius Press, 1987), 209.

7. *Basic Writings of St. Augustine*, vol. 1, ed. Whitney Oates (New York: Random House, 1948), 378–379.

Chapter 4

1. Donald and Idella Gallagher, eds., *The Education of Man: The Educational Philosophy of Jacques Maritain* (Garden City, N.Y.: Doubleday, 1962). Most of Maritain's lectures and essays on education are also published in a French edition, *Pour une philosophie de l'éducation* (Paris: Fayard, 1959). See also, James V. Schall, *Jacques Maritain: The Philosopher in Society* (Lanham, Md.: Rowman & Littlefield, 1998).

2. Maritain, *Education at the Crossroads*, 30–31.

3. Ibid., 32.

4. Ibid,. 93–94.

5. Ibid., 94. "Christian faith knows that human nature is good in itself but has been put out of order by original sin; hence it sees that Christian education will recognize the necessity of a stern discipline, and even of a certain fear, on the condition that this discipline, instead of being merely external—and futile—should appeal to the understanding and the will of the child and become self-discipline, and that the fear should be respect and reverence, not blind animal dread. And Christian faith knows that supernatural grace matters more than original sin, and the weakness of

human nature, for grace heals and superelevates nature and makes man participator in divine life itself; hence it is that Christian education will never lose sight of the God-given equipment of virtues and gifts through which eternal life begins here below," Maritain, *The Education of Man*, 131.

6. Ibid., 74.
7. Gallagher, *The Education of Man*, 154–158.
8. Charles M. Schulz, *Nobody's Perfect, Charlie Brown* (New York: Fawcett, 1963).
9. Maritain, *Education at the Crossroads*, 64.
10. Gallagher, *The Education of Man*, 154.
11. Ibid, 154–155.
12. Ibid., 155.
13. Ibid., 156–157.
14. Ibid., 157.
15. Ibid., 158.
16. Ibid.
17. Ibid., 41.
18. Ibid., 129.
19. Ibid., 130.
20. Maritain, *Education at the Crossroads*, 29.
21. Ibid., 30.
22. Gallagher, *The Education of Man*, 116.
23. Maritain, *Education at the Crossroads*, 84.
24. Ibid., 85–86.
25. Jacques Maritain, *Notebooks*, trans. Joseph Evans (Albany, N.Y.: Magi Books, 1984), 133.
26. Ibid., 290–297.
27. Ibid., 134.
28. Ibid., 135.
29. Ibid., 136.
30. Ibid., 136–137.
31. Maritain, *Education at the Crossroads*, 39.

Chapter 5

1. G. K. Chesterton, *A Short History of England* (New York: Phoenix Library, 1951), 59.

2. *Basic Writings of Augustine*, vol. 1, 101.

3. Charles M. Schulz, *If Beagles Could Fly* (New York: Topper, 1990).

4. Flannery O'Connor, *The Habit of Being* (New York: Vintage, 1979), 307.

5. James V. Schall, *Unexpected Meditations Late in the XXth Century* (Chicago: Franciscan Herald Press, 1985).

6. Hilaire Belloc, *Hills and the Sea* (Marlboro, Vt.: Marlboro Press, 1906 [Reprint]).

7. Ibid., 187–188.

8. Boswell, *Life of Johnson*, II: 404.

9. *Josef Pieper: An Anthology* (San Francisco: Ignatius Press, 1989), 33.

10. Ibid., 35.

11. Thomas à Kempis, *Sermons to the Novices Regular*, trans. Vincent Scully (London: Kegan Paul, Trench, Trübner, and Co., 1909), 41–42.

12. James V. Schall, "On the Neglect of Hell in Political Theory," in *The Politics of Heaven and Hell: Christian Themes from Classical, Medieval, and Modern Political Philosophy* (Lanham, Md.: University Press of America, 1984), 83–106.

13. Josef Pieper, *Enthusiasm and the Divine Madness: On the Platonic Dialogue "Phaedrus"* (New York: Harcourt, 1964).

14. E.F. Schumacher, *A Guide for the Perplexed* (New York: Harper Colophon, 1977), 132.

Chapter 6

1. Jennifer Roback Morse, "The Modern State as an Occasion of Sin," *Notre Dame Journal of Law, Ethics, & Public Policy* 11, no. 2 (1997): 548.

Chapter 7

1. Charles M. Schulz, *Could You Be More Pacific?* (New York: Topper Books, 1991).

2. Boswell, *Life of Johnson*, I: 499.

3. Humphrey Carpenter, ed., *The Letters of J. R. R. Tolkien* (Boston: Houghton-Mifflin, 1981), 400.

Interlude IV

1. John Paul II, *Crossing the Threshold of Hope* (New York: Knopf, 1994), 36.
2. Paul Johnson, *Intellectuals* (New York: Harper and Row, 1988).

Chapter 8

1. Samuel Johnson, *Rasselas; Poems, and Selected Prose,* ed. B. Bronson (New York: Holt, Rinehart, and Winston, 1958), 463.
2. I have argued this point more fully in *At the Limits of Political Philosophy: From "Brilliant Errors" to Things of Uncommon Importance* (Washington, D.C.: The Catholic University of America Press, 1996) and *Reason, Revelation and the Foundations of Political Philosophy* (Baton Rouge, La.: Louisiana State University Press, 1987).
3. Leo Strauss, *Persecution and the Art of Writing* (Westport, Conn.: Greenwood, 1952), 22–37.
4. See James V. Schall, "A Meditation on Evil," *The Aquinas Review* 7, no. 1 (2000): 25–42.
5. See James V. Schall, "Aristotle on Friendship," *The Classical Bulletin* 65, nos. 3 & 4 (1989): 82–97.
6. Recently, I came across a book by Gene Fendt and David Rozema that makes this point in another way: *Plato's Enemies: Plato, a Kind of Poet* (Westport, Conn.: Greenwood, 1998).
7. See *Conversations with Eric Voegelin,* ed. R. Eric O'Connor (Montreal: Thomas More Institute, 1980); G. K. Chesterton, *Orthodoxy* (San Francisco: Ignatius Press, 1986).
8. I refer here to "Schall's List of Books to Keep Sane By," in *Another Sort of Learning* or in *A Student's Guide to Liberal Learning.* See also the Appendix to this volume for a slightly different sort of book list.
9. Strauss, *Liberalism: Ancient and Modern,* Chapter 1.
10. See *Josef Pieper: An Anthology.*

11. Wilhelmsen, "Great Books: Enemies of Wisdom?" 331.

12. Leo Strauss, *The City and Man* (Chicago: University of Chicago Press, 1964), 8.

13. Boswell, *Life of Johnson*, I: 413. This idea of being unable to carry out what was known naturally of virtue was also Augustine's. See Charles N. R. McCoy, *The Structure of Political Thought* (New York: McGraw-Hill, 1963), 118.

Chapter 9

1. Bernard Schwerbaum, *The New Yorker*, April 30, 1990.

2. *Conversations with Eric Voegelin*, 32–33.

3. See James V. Schall, "The Christian Guardians," in *The Politics of Heaven and Hell: Christian Themes from Classical, Medieval, and Modern Political Philosophy*, 67–82.

4. Hepin, *The New Yorker*, November 12, 1990.

5. *Lettres de Madame de Sévigné à sa fille et à ses amis* (Paris: A. Belin, 1812), III, 260.

6. L'Amour, *The Education of a Wandering Man*, 3.

7. Boswell, *Life of Johnson*, II: 122.

8. Ibid., 124.

9. Ibid., 124–125.

10. T. H. White, *The Once and Future King* (New York: Ace, 1987), 55.

11. Robert Fulghum, *All I Need to Know I Learned in Kindergarten: Uncommon Thoughts on Common Things* (New York: Ivy Books, 1988), 116–117.

12. Schumacher, *A Guide for the Perplexed*, 61–79.

13. Denis de Rougemont, *Love in the Western World*, trans. Montgomery Belgion (New York: Schocken, 1983).

Chapter 10

1. O'Connor, *The Habit of Being*, 353–354; *Selected Essays of Hilaire Belloc* (London: Methuen, 1948), 48–52.

2. James V. Schall, S. J., *The Distinctiveness of Christianity* (San Francisco: Ignatius Press, 1982), 277.

3. *Josef Pieper: An Anthology*, 33.

Chapter 11

1.   Alasdair MacIntyre, *After Virtue* (Notre Dame: University of Notre Dame Press, 1981), 238.

2.   *Conversations with Eric Voegelin*, 6.

3.   Robert L. Short, *The Parables of Peanuts* (New York: Harper, 1968), 132.

4.   G. K. Chesterton, *Orthodoxy* (Garden City, N.Y.: Doubleday Image, 1959), 160.

5.   Boswell, *Life of Johnson*, II: 221.

6.   Jay Tolson, ed., *The Correspondence of Shelby Foote & Walker Percy* (New York: Doubleday, 1997), 14–15.

7.   Mell Lazarus, *Miss Peach* (New York: Grosset & Dunlap, 1972).

8.   Leo Strauss, "What Is Political Philosophy?" in *What Is Political Philosophy? And Other Studies* (Glencoe, Ill.: The Free Press, 1959), 39.

Bibliography

Arkes, Hadley. *First Things: An Inquiry into the First Principles of Morals and Justice.* Princeton: Princeton University Press, 1986.

Augustine. *Basic Writings of St. Augustine.* Two vols. Edited by Whitney Oates. New York: Random House, 1948.

Balthasar, Hans Urs von. *A Short Primer for Unsettled Laymen.* Translated by Mary Skerry. San Francisco: Ignatius Press, 1980.

Belloc, Hilaire. *The Four Men.* Oxford: Oxford University Press, 1984.

_____. *Hilaire Belloc: Stories, Essays, and Poems.* Edited by J. B. Morton. London: Dent, 1938.

_____. *Hills and the Sea.* New York: Scribner's, 1906.

_____. *Miniatures of French History.* LaSalle, Ill.: Sherwood Sugden, 1990.

_____. *The Path to Rome.* Garden City, N.Y.: Doubleday Image, 1956.

_____. *Selected Essays of Hilaire Belloc.* Edited by J. B. Morton. London: Methuen, 1948.

Berry, Wendell. *A Place on Earth.* Rev. ed. New York: North Point, 1983.

_____. *Jayber Crow: The Life Story of Jayber Crow, Barber, of the Port William Membership, as Written by Himself: A Novel.* Washington D.C.: Counterpoint, 2000.

Bloom, Allan. *The Closing of the American Mind.* New York: Simon & Schuster, 1987.

Bochenski, J. M. *Philosophy: An Introduction.* New York: Harper Torchbooks, 1972.

Boswell, James. *Life of Johnson.* 2 vols. Oxford: Oxford University Press, 1931.

_____. *Boswell on the Grand Tour: Germany and Switzerland, 1764.* Edited by Frederick A. Pottle. New York: McGraw & Hill, 1953.

Butterfield, Herbert. *Christianity and History.* London: Fontana, 1964.

Camus, Albert. *Lyrical and Critical Essays.* Edited by Philip Thody. New York: Vintage, 1968.

Chesterton, G. K. *A Short History of England.* New York: Phoenix Library, 1951.

_____. *The More Quotable Chesterton.* Edited by George Marlin and others. San Francisco: Ignatius Press, 1988.

_____. *Orthodoxy.* Garden City, N.Y.: Doubleday Image, 1959.

_____. *St. Thomas Aquinas.* Garden City, N.Y.: Doubleday Image, 1956.

_____. *What's Wrong with the World.* San Francisco: Ignatius Press, 1994.

Dawson, Christopher. *Religion and the Rise of Western Culture.* Garden City, N. Y.: Doubleday Image. 1956.

Derrick, Christopher. *Escape from Scepticism: Liberal Education as if the Truth Really Mattered.* LaSalle, Ill..: Sherwood Sugden, 1977.

_____. *Joy Without a Cause.* LaSalle, Ill.: Sherwood Sugden, 1979.

Fendt, Gene, and David Rozema. *Plato's Enemies: Plato, a Kind of Poet.* Westport, Conn.: Greenwood, 1998.

Fulghum, Robert. *All I Need to Know I Learned in Kindergarten: Uncommon Thoughts on Common Things.* New York: Ivy Books, 1988.

Gilson, Etienne. *The Unity of Philosophical Experience.* San Francisco: Ignatius Press, 1999.

Huizinga, Johan. *Homo Ludens: A Study of the Play Element in Culture.* Boston: Beacon Press, 1959.

Jaki, Stanley. *Chance or Reality and Other Essays.* Wilmington, Del.: Intercollegiate Studies Institute, 1986.

_____. *The Road of Science and the Ways to God.* Chicago: University of Chicago Press, 1978.

John Paul II. *Crossing the Threshold of Hope.* New York: Knopf, 1994.

Johnson, Paul. *Intellectuals.* New York: Harper, 1988.

Johnson, Samuel. *Rassalas, Poems, and Selected Prose.* Edited by B. Bronson. New York: Holt, 1958.

Kass, Leon. *The Hungry Soul: Eating and the Perfection of Our Nature.* Chicago: University of Chicago Press, 1999.

à Kempis, Thomas. *Sermons to the Novices Regular.* Translated by Vincent Scully. London: Kegan Paul, Trench, Trübner, and Co., 1909.

Kreeft, Peter. *Back to Virtue.* San Francisco: Ignatius Press, 1992.

_____. *C. S. Lewis for the Third Millennium.* San Francisco: Ignatius Press, 1994.

L'Amour, Louis. *Education of a Wandering Man.* New York: Bantam, 1990.

Lazarus, Mell. *Miss Peach.* New York: Grosset & Dunlap, 1972.

Lewis, C. S. *The Abolition of Man.* New York: Macmillan, 1947.

_____. *Mere Christianity.* New York: Macmillan, 1952.

_____. *Surprised by Joy: The Shape of My Early Life.* New York: Harcourt, 1955.

_____. *The Weight of Glory and Other Addresses.* New York: Macmillan, 1980.

MacIntyre, Alasdair. *After Virtue.* Notre Dame, Ind.: University of Notre Dame Press, 1981.

Maritain, Jacques. *Education at the Crossroads.* New Haven, Conn.: Yale University Press, 1943.

_____. *The Education of Man: The Educational Philosophy of Jacques Maritain.* Edited by Donald and Idella Gallagher. Garden City, N.Y.: Doubleday, 1962.

_____. *Notebooks.* Translated by Joseph Evans. Albany, N.Y.: Magi Books, 1984.

Maritain, Raïssa. *Raïssa's Journal.* Albany, N.Y.: Magi Books, 1974.

Mascall, E. L. *The Christian Universe.* London: Darton, Longman & Todd, 1966.

McCoy, Charles N. R. *The Structure of Political Thought.* New York: McGraw-Hill, 1963.

McDonald, Wesley. "Recovering a Neglected Conservative Mind." *University Bookman* 34, no. 4 (1994): 19–20

McInerny, Ralph. *St. Thomas Aquinas.* Notre Dame, Ind.: University of Notre Dame Press, 1977.

Morse, Jennifer Roback. "The Modern State as an Occasion of Sin." *Notre Dame Journal of Law, Ethics, & Public Policy* 11, no. 2 (1997).

Mother Teresa. *Love: A Fruit Always in Season: Daily Meditations of Mother Teresa.* Edited by Dorothy Hunt. San Francisco: Ignatius Press, 1987.

O'Connor, Flannery. *The Habit of Being.* Edited by Sally Fitzgerald. New York: Vintage, 1979.

Percy, Walker. *Conversations with Walker Percy.* Edited by Lewis A. Lawson and Victor Kramer. Oxford, Miss.: University Press of Mississippi, 1985.

Pickstock, Catherine. *After Writing: On the Liturgical Consummation of Philosophy.* Oxford: Blackwell, 1998.

Pieper, Josef. *Enthusiasm and the Divine Madness: On the Platonic Dialogue "Phaedrus."* Translated by Richard and Clara Winston. New York: Harcourt, 1964.

_____. *Faith, Hope, Love.* San Francisco: Ignatius Press, 1997.

_____. *Guide to Thomas Aquinas.* Translated by Richard and Clara Winston. San Francisco: Ignatius Press, 1991.

_____. *In Defense of Philosophy.* Translated by Lothar Krauth. San Francisco: Ignatius Press, 1992.

_____. *In Search of the Sacred.* Translated by Lothar Krauth. San Francisco: Ignatius Press, 1991.

_____. *In Tune with the World: A Theory of Festivity.* Chicago: Franciscan Herald Press, 1973.

_____. *Living the Truth: The Truth of All Things and Reality and the Good.* San Francisco: Ignatius Press, 1989.

_____. *Josef Pieper: An Anthology.* San Francisco: Ignatius Press, 1989.

_____. *Leisure: The Basis of Culture.* Translated by Alexander Dru. New York: Pantheon, 1952.

Rougemont, Denis de. *Love in the Western World.* Translated by Montgomery Belgion. New York: Schocken, 1983.

Sayers, Dorothy. *The Whimsical Christian.* New York: Macmillan, 1978.

Schall, James V. *Another Sort of Learning.* San Francisco: Ignatius Press, 1988.

_____. "Aristotle on Friendship," *The Classical Bulletin* 65 (1989): 82–97.

_____. *At the Limits of Political Philosophy: From "Brilliant Errors" to Things of Uncommon Importance.* Washington, D.C.: The Catholic University of America Press, 1996.

_____. *The Distinctiveness of Christianity*. San Francisco: Ignatius Press, 1982.

_____. *Does Catholicism Still Exist?* Staten Island, N.Y.: Alba House, 1994.

_____. *Idylls and Rambles: Lighter Christian Essays*. San Francisco: Ignatius Press, 1994.

_____. *Jacques Maritain: The Philosopher in Society*. Lanham, Md.: Rowman & Littlefield, 1998.

_____. "A Meditation on Evil," *The Aquinas Review* 7, no. 1 (2000): 25–42.

_____. *The Politics of Heaven and Hell: Christian Themes from Classical, Medieval, and Modern Political Philosophy*. Lanham, Md.: University Press of America, 1984.

_____. *The Praise of "Sons of Bitches": On the Worship of God by Fallen Men*. Slough, England: St. Paul Publications, 1978.

_____. *Reason, Revelation and the Foundations of Political Philosophy*. Baton Rouge, La.: Louisiana State University Press, 1987.

_____. *Redeeming the Time*. New York: Sheed & Ward, 1968.

_____. *Religion, Wealth, and Poverty*. Vancouver: Fraser Institute, 1990.

_____. *Schall on Chesterton*. Washington: The Catholic University of America Press, 2000.

_____. *A Student's Guide to Liberal Learning*. Wilmington, Del.: ISI Books, 2000.

_____. *Unexpected Meditations Late in the XXth Century*. Chicago: Franciscan Herald Press, 1985.

_____. *What Is God Like?* Collegeville, Minn.: Michael Glazer/Liturgical Press, 1992.

Schulz, Charles. *Could You Be More Pacific?* New York: Topper Books, 1991.

_____. *If Beagles Could Fly*. New York: Topper Books, 1979.

_____. *Nobody's Perfect, Charlie Brown*. New York: Fawcett, 1963.

Schumacher, E. F. *A Guide for the Perplexed*. New York: Harper Colophon, 1977.

Short, Robert L. *The Parables of Peanuts*. New York: Harper, 1968.

Simon, Julian. *The Ultimate Resource II*. Princeton, N.J.: Princeton University Press, 1996.

Simon, Yves. *A General Theory of Authority*. Notre Dame, Ind.: University of Notre Dame Press, 1980.

Sokolowski, Robert. *The God of Faith and Reason.* Washington: The Catholic University of America Press, 1995.

Strauss, Leo. *The City and Man.* Chicago: University of Chicago Press, 1964.

_____. *Liberalism: Ancient and Modern.* New York: Basic Books, 1968.

_____. *Persecution and the Art of Writing.* Westport, Conn.: Greenwood, 1952.

_____. *What Is Political Philosophy? And Other Studies.* Glencoe, Ill.: The Free Press, 1959.

Tolkien, J. R. R. *The Letters of J. R. R. Tolkien.* Edited by Humphrey Carpenter. Boston: Houghton-Mifflin, 1981.

_____. *The Tolkien Reader.* New York: Ballantine, 1966.

Tolson, Jay, ed. *The Correspondence of Shelby Foote & Walker Percy.* New York: Doubleday, 1997.

Tuchman, Barbara. *A Distant Mirror: The Calamitous Fourteenth Century.* New York: Ballantine, 1978.

Veatch, Henry. *Rational Man: A Modern Interpretation of Aristotelian Ethics.* Bloomington, Ind.: Indiana University Press, 1966.

Voegelin, Eric. *Conversations with Eric Voegelin.* Edited by R. Eric O'Connor. Montreal: Thomas More Institute Press, 1980.

Waugh, Evelyn. *Brideshead Revisited.* Boston: Little, Brown & Co., 1948.

White, T. H. *The Once and Future King.* New York: Ace, 1987.

Wilhelmsen, Frederick D. "Great Books: Enemies of Wisdom?" *Modern Age* 31 (Summer/Fall, 1987): 323–331.

_____. *The Paradoxical Structure of Existence.* Albany, N.Y.: Preserving Christian Publications, 1995.

Woznicki, Andrew N. *Karol Wojtyla's Existential Personalism.* New Britain, Conn.: Mariel, 1980.

Index